THE NEWCASTLE
& CARLISLE RAILWAY

THE NEWCASTLE
& CARLISLE RAILWAY

G. WHITTLE

DAVID & CHARLES

Newton Abbot London North Pomfret (Vt)

British Library Cataloguing in Publication Data

Whittle, George
   The Newcastle & Carlisle Railway.
1. Newcastle and Carlisle Railway—History
I. Title
385'.09427   HE3020.N/

ISBN 0–7153–7855–4

Photoset and printed in Great Britain
by REDWOOD BURN LIMITED
Trowbridge and Esher
for David & Charles (Publishers) Limited
Brunel House Newton Abbot Devon

Published in the United States of America
by David & Charles Inc
North Pomfret Vermont 05053 USA

Contents

Introduction and Acknowledgements

The Newcastle & Carlisle Railway is one of Britain's earliest railways, and crosses England's narrowest point in the extreme north of the country. Branches were gradually added to the original cross-country line, but in the last two decades, as might be expected, railway contraction has meant most of them have gone. At one point in the 1960s even the N & CR itself was under threat, and although such important lines, not too far distant, as the Stainmore line, the Waverley route, and Dumfries–Stranraer, were axed, the N & CR survived.

The atmosphere of Northumbria and East Cumberland is distinctive, and the people and scenery outstanding; I hope I have portrayed enough to reflect the character of the area. In the railway context, visualise such places as Reedsmouth, Bellingham, Lambley, Langley, or beside Stephenson's house at Wylam, when the railways were busy and part of local life, and visit such places now, and reflect. Go to Cowran Hills cutting, and watch a diesel-hauled train, and it does not really need much imagination to reflect the early years of the line. The N & CR still shows much of its early independence and the thought of its closure and removal seems sacrilegious.

Inevitably, with a long history, there is much that could be put into a book such as this, far more than could be included economically here. I hope readers will feel that the history is fairly well covered, and that the continuity from the 1820s to the present time blends in within the overall story.

A great number of people have provided assistance in the production of a book which really started in 1966 when I began an MA at Queen's University, Belfast. This thesis, in the geography department of the University, is an important adjunct to the book, and I offer thanks to the former head of department, Professor E. Estyn Evans, and to my supervisor, Dr Robert Common. The former BTC records in York (W. MacDonald) and Edinburgh (R. M. Hogg) gave invaluable assistance. Much is owed also to two books, J. S. Maclean's *Newcastle & Carlisle Railway* of 1948, and Tomlinson's *North Eastern Railway*. Frank Graham's reprint of Carmichael's *Views on the Newcastle & Carlisle Railway* also deserves special mention.

I can but list others who have helped, and tender apologies to anyone I may have omitted inadvertently: the Public Record Office; Newcastle-upon-Tyne city library; K. Hoole; John Thomas; the NCB (Gateshead); J. Dolan; I. S. Carr; Brian Webb; M. Phillips; the Stormont Library (Belfast); M. F. Barbey; the Cumbrian County Archives; BR Public Relations Department (Newcastle); the late Mrs Maralyn Hubbard; P. Bernard; David Jones and Len Hoyland. In the Northumbrian Fells I recall help in specific information from A. J. V. Bickerton of Barrasford and W. A. Benson of Newbrough. Last, but not least, my thanks to M. J. Frost, MSC, FRGS, Dr J. Appleton of Hull University, to my parents, and to my good friend, Miss Carole West and to Miss Cathy Townsend for help with the index.

G. WHITTLE

CHAPTER 1

The Beginnings

"I have not a doubt that a Railway joined to the Carlisle
Canal would benefit the trade of the latter in a greater degree than the same line of connexion with Newcastle
would, if made by Canal"—Josias Jessop, 1825

Canal Plans

In 1756 when Newcastle and Carlisle were still connected only
by a bridle way, the army's Marshall Wade began making the
military road westwards from Newcastle, for 30 miles following
the line of the Emperor Hadrian's Wall to Greenhead. This work
was an aftermath of the '45 Rebellion in Scotland. A later improvement of the transport system was the Hexham–Haydon
Bridge–Haltwhistle turnpike road.

1776 was the year of the first serious consideration of a Newcastle–Carlisle canal to allow easier trade across this narrowest
neck of England. Ralph Dodd planned a canal to link the Tyne at
Newcastle with the Solway Firth at Maryport, via Carlisle and
Hexham. The route of the canal was mainly on the south side of
the river Tyne, west of Newcastle. Dodd's scheme was the first of
many. John Sutcliffe, an engineer, also surveyed for a canal and
made certain objections to Dodd's route. Then from Ireland
came William Chapman in 1794, who promptly devoted his attention to the canal idea which by this time was uppermost in the
minds of many industrialists and tradespeople of the Tyneside
region. Chapman's first route for a canal was similar to that of
Dodd in beginning at Newcastle and ending at Maryport, but
there the similarity ended. The main difference lay in a route
mainly on the north side of the Tyne and the east end was at a

proposed dock at Ouseburn, at the east end of Newcastle. One of Chapman's helpers was another engineer, Josias Jessop. In February 1797 Robert Whitworth, yet another engineer, examined the Chapman and Sutcliffe canal routes and suggested alterations. He favoured a route south of the Tyne. Meanwhile, certain coal owners of the Tyneside area raised objections to Chapman's canal and said they would oppose it. Chapman modified the plan and a Bill was deposited in Parliament for a Newcastle to Haydon Bridge canal, which would primarily serve the lead industry south of the latter place, and the town of Hexham. Even this met great opposition, and it was withdrawn by its promoters. It seems that there were many who opposed a canal, despite the apparent trade advantages any canal in the Tyne valley or across to Carlisle would bring. One of the many objectors to the Haydon Bridge Bill was the Vicar of St John Lee, Hexham, and his flock who "feared that the canal at the foot of the hill on which the Church stood would endanger its safety"! The opposition did not deter Chapman, who continued for many years to consider Tyne–Solway canal routes; he had issued six such reports by 1798.

A whisper of the future was heard in 1800. In February of that year William Thomas of Denton Hall, near Newcastle, read a paper to a learned society proposing an adaptation of the old waggonways for passenger and general traffic between Newcastle and Hexham. This was not taken very seriously at the time; waggonways, of which there were a number in North East colliery areas including Tyneside, were primitive in their evolution, and horse haulage was the rule. It was only from about 1813–14 that the steam locomotive began to be seriously considered for hauling wagons; George Stephenson built and tried out his first locomotive at Killingworth, north of Newcastle, during 1814. The success of the early locomotives undoubtedly made the waggonway or railway a more obvious form of communication and transport than it had been.

In 1808 Thomas Telford, one of the country's top engineers, made a Newcastle–Solway canal survey. Again, great discussion and argument followed but still nothing was done, in this case because of the French war still in progress. After Waterloo in 1815, attention returned to the canal, but the influence of waggonways was growing. Meanwhile a Solway Firth–Carlisle canal was constructed, opening in 1823, which raised the question of extending it for the 60 miles to Newcastle. William Chapman, the great canal champion, declared himself in favour of a railway, stating that his 1796 canal route would suit a railway. Undoubtedly Chapman's declaration raised the level of discussion to almost a furore, and matters reached their head. Action was necessary.

The problem now, in view of Chapman's declaration for a railway, was to decide whether a Newcastle–Carlisle railway or a canal would be the better plan.

On 21 August 1824 the High Sheriff of Northumberland convened and presided over a county meeting in Newcastle, to consider the scheme of "a communication by railways between Newcastle and Carlisle". The Stockton to Darlington Railway project at this period helped to implant the railway idea in the minds of many. The Newcastle meeting ended in a committee of inquiry being appointed to report on the best means of improving the communication between Newcastle and Carlisle—largely because of Mr William Armstrong's plea imploring "the meeting to reject their spiritless proposition for a railroad".

William Chapman, the canal engineer who now favoured a railway, was chosen to report on the costs and advantages of either a ship canal or a railroad between Newcastle and Carlisle. His report is of the greatest importance as it undoubtedly spurred on the hesitating pressure towards a railway. Chapman's report was dated 27 October 1824, and estimated the cost of a canal at £888,000, and a railway at £252,488. The course he recommended for the railway ran from the west end of the Close at Newcastle, along the north bank of the Tyne to Newburn, across the river to Ryton Haughs, and thence via Hexham, Haydon Bridge, Haltwhistle, and on the north side of the river Irthing past Lanercost Priory, crossing the river near Ruleholme

11

and on to Carlisle. The course deliberately avoided the estates of the Earl of Carlisle at Naworth Castle, the Earl being probably the most important person and landowner between Newcastle and Carlisle. Undoubtedly Chapman's report further increased the number of supporters for a railway, and further diminished the canal supporters. Regarding the canal plan he stated the cost involved would "show to any dispassionate mind the impropriety of any longer entertaining the idea of a ship canal".

The "Committee of Enquiry to inquire into the practicability of improving the existing communication between Newcastle and Carlisle" engaged further eminent engineers to consider the route for a railway, to assess the best possible line. One engineer, Benjamin Thompson, produced a plan in November 1825. His proposed route ran from Newcastle, and crossed the Tyne at Scotswood, to Blaydon, proceeding westwards on the south side of the river to Hexham. A bridge over the Tyne at Tyne Green, just west of Hexham, took the line to the north bank, crossing the North Tyne east of Warden, and remaining on the north side of the South Tyne to Haltwhistle. The route then was similar to Chapman's, up the Tipalt gap, and across the Irthing at Upper Denton, following Chapman's route to Carlisle. A branch line ran to Brampton. Another engineer, Josias Jessop, had reported to the committee on 4 March 1825 and his findings more-or-less ended hopes of the remaining canal promoters. He found that a railway would cost a third of a canal. His report is worth quoting in some detail, as it led immediately to the formation of the railway company:

> I have examined the country between Newcastle and Carlisle, following the general direction of the vallies [sic] of the South Tyne, Tipple, Irthing and Eden, for the purpose of ascertaining whether a canal or a railway is the best medium of internal communication between the above-named places; If it was a simple unconnected question which mode of communication is preferable for general purposes, that is, to convey articles of trade and commerce of every description from one point to another, I would have little hesitation in saying that a railway is the best, as it not only requires less capital to complete it but also will convey merchandise more cheaply and

expeditiously and with equal safety; but supposing it to form only part of a communication between the German Ocean and the Irish Sea, the Tyne having to be navigated at the east end, and the Carlisle Canal at the west, other reasons will influence the decision of the question, of which this is the principle [sic] one—whether a Canal will occasion such an increase of trade beyond what would be conveyed by a Railway, added to the advantage of avoiding twice changing the carriage, as will compensate for the excess of capital, and the additional expense of conveyance. From all that I can learn of the nature of the trade, I am of the opinion that it cannot; so far from it, I am disposed to think that not only as much, but more will pass by a Railway than by a Canal, as the facility afforded by a Railway of making Branches from either side, will not only extend the present sources, but will also induce individuals to open collieries, mines and quarries, from which they can send the produce at once to its destination without the inconvenience of removal, and more cheaply, as they will not have to defray the interest of capital which would probably prevent a distant trade in articles of low value, that would only have its origin in the facility of making a connexion with so simple and cheap a mode of conveyance as a Railway. I have not a doubt, for the foregoing reasons, that a Railway joined to the Carlisle Canal would benefit the trade of the latter in a greater degree than the same line of connexion with Newcastle would, if made by Canal.

The Newcastle & Carlisle Railroad

Events swiftly followed Jessop's report. On 26 March 1825 the "committee" transformed itself into the "Newcastle-on-Tyne and Carlisle Railroad Company". The High Sheriff of Northumberland was Chairman, and there were 24 directors. On 28 March the Prospectus was issued, informing the public that the new company was to have a capital of £300,000. There was an immediate response—by 6 May 1825 the whole of the sum had been subscribed for by the sale of shares (at £100 each). Thus is seen the wide support for the project.

The Prospectus declared that "the expense of executing the work has been estimated at £252,488; to this estimate Mr Jessop has thought it right to make an addition of £40,000 on account of the advance in the price of iron and some other circumstances—making in the whole £292,488 which includes an allowance of no less a sum than £32,933 for incidents and unforeseen expenses. The capital required for the undertaking is £300,000, divided into 3,000 shares of £100 each, of which one-sixth part is reserved for the landowners through which the line passes."

The lucrative picture conjured up by the Prospectus is worth quoting from:

> It may with confidence be asserted that there are few, if any, situations in Great Britain which present a surer prospect of success to such an undertaking; there are no existing Canal Interests to interfere with or to be injured by the proposed Railroad, the country on both sides of the line abounds in lead, coal, lime and other mineral productions, the transit of which on different portions of the line, independent of that of merchandise from one extremity to the other, has been estimated to produce a revenue sufficient to compensate those who may engage in the undertaking. At the same time, imperfect as is the present medium of communication, the carriage of merchandise between Newcastle and Carlisle is so considerable as to justify the confident expectation of a large additional return from that source.

The N & CR directors, headed by John George Lambton, later Earl of Durham, were appointed on 9 April 1825, and held their first meeting at Newcastle on 23 April.

William Chapman reported for a second time to the N & CR on 16 June 1825, on a route for the railway. An important point in this report was his view on locomotive traction. He did not recommend their use unless "much improved beyond what they were. They are objectionable in various ways. In the first place, gentlemen through whose estates or near whose residences they pass, object to their appearance and the noise and smoke rising from them. Whilst new, and on level planes, they possess advantages in expedition; but by their quick motion and that degree of shaking which cannot be avoided, they in the end require so much and frequent repairs as to render their advantage dubious; exclusive of their being unfitted to receive and discharge the carriages that are wanted to be taken forward, and sent off aside in such places of the line as do not coincide with their stages or feeding places."

The directors were now desirous of achieving the best route for their line. In this respect Benjamin Thompson was called in, while Chapman and Jessop continued to give their ideas. The line was intended to be operated completely by horses, as locomotives or fixed engines were considered "incompatible with the design of a public railway which was to be used by carriers of all kinds under stated conditions like a common highway". In October 1825 there was reported a scheme to build a branch line from Brampton to Annan, Dumfriesshire, certain landowners offering to give the necessary land "without any compensation whatsoever". There was, however, no support for this.

At this time the N & CR was holding discussions with landowners along the projected route, and was finding some objectors to its passage. It was not going to be a simple matter to fix the route. In December the directors proposed seven short branch lines to add to the main line.

These were as follows:

1. Elswick to Thornton Street, Newcastle "for the accommodation of the high part of Newcastle".
2. Scotswood to Lemington Glass Works and colliery waggonways of Wylam and Holywell, "passing by various Manufactories, Tile and Brick works".
3. Scotswood Bridge to Swalwell "to receive coals coming down the Vale of Derwent and for the convenience of the manufacturing and populous town of Swalwell".
4. To Brampton. "Branches serving that town will bring down the coals and lime of Tindale Fell and Hartley Burn for the supply of Carlisle and a very wide district."
5. "A short turn out of the Main Line for the accommodation of Hexham."
6,7. "strike into Carlisle at different points."

It is perhaps worth stating that eventually when the N & CR obtained its Act, only the first branch was included.

Alternatives and Alterations

One of the largest landowners in the Haydon Bridge district, the Greenwich Hospital Commissioners, employed George Stephenson to survey the north side of the Tyne from near Hexham eastwards, to provide an alternative to the N&CR routes of Thompson, Chapman and Jessop. Joseph Locke levelled Stephenson's line. It began by Warden Bridge, west of Hexham, and passed by means of a 440yd tunnel under the hill behind the Hermitage, past the north end of Hexham road bridge, to Corbridge and by a $1\frac{3}{4}$-mile inclined plane up the valley side at 1 in 36. It then ran past Heddon-on-the-Wall, to the south-west corner of Newcastle's Town Moor and by a $1\frac{1}{4}$-mile incline (1 in 48) to the quay by the Ouseburn, at the east end of Newcastle. This line was $23\frac{1}{2}$ miles long, and Benjamin Thompson's route for this section was $24\frac{1}{4}$ miles. George Stephenson also examined the N & CR line route, and found some serious errors in its levels, so that on 12 February 1826 the directors felt that their scheme was in no position yet to be put into Parliament.

The Earl of Carlisle's agents also suggested a revision of the route, near Brampton. They suggested that if the N & CR took a more southerly course hereabouts, it could pass by the Brampton coal staiths and obviate the need for a branch line. Mr Chapman however found that such a revision would require inclined planes. It seems also, that many citizens of Brampton opposed the N & CR passing through, fearing it would "ruin" the town. John Studholme, of Carlisle, surveyed an alternative route from Carlisle to the Gilsland area, which followed a completely different route from all earlier suggestions. Studholme's line left Carlisle, passing north of Scotby, Wetheral and Corby, through the village of Hayton, to the south of Naworth park through Upper Denton and south of Mumps Hall. It would pass on $1\frac{1}{2}$ miles south of Brampton, instead of north of that small town. The Earl of Carlisle liked the plan, and at a meeting in Newcastle on 7 June 1827, the route was adopted by the N & CR.

There were then a few other alterations in the area: a south-

16

ward alteration near Talkin Tarn to avoid an inclined plane; and a similar shift at Hayton to avoid the home of Sir Hew Dalrymple Ross "who objected to the railway being carried past his house at Hayton, requiring as the price of his consent to this invasion of his privacy, the sum of £8,000".

The course of the line was fixed on 8 April 1828, and the following day the parliamentary survey was begun by T. O. Blackett at the east end and by Studholme at the west end. The plans were ready in August, and the notice of application to Parliament was sent in during November. The line thus ran from the west of the Close, Newcastle, to the summit level near Gilsland as before, and then by Upper Denton and Wetheral to the Canal Basin, Carlisle. The Thornton Street branch was included. The steepest gradient was 1 in 107; the least 1 in 2263.

But the N & CR was not yet out of the wood as far as difficulties with landowners were concerned. There were in 1828, still 35 who objected to the line passing through their lands. Certain of them were proving extremely intractable, but none more so than Mr Charles Bacon, of Styford Hall, Riding Mill.

Mr Charles Bacon

The Bacon saga fully occupied the directors' attention for some considerable time. Every approach to Charles Bacon was stonewalled—he would *not* sell any of his land to the N & CR at any price. He did not like nor want to see a railway near his home. Unfortunately, his lands straddled the Tyne Valley, and except by huge engineering expenses it was impossible to avoid them. Mr Bacon exasperated the N & CR. On 17 February 1829 the company issued a pamphlet to its supporters and the public, explaining the status quo with Mr Bacon whilst cleverly praising 'co-operative' landowners to show him up:

> The line must necessarily approach more nearly than would be wished to the seats of some of the County Gentlemen; but they have not permitted their private feelings to interfere with the obvious interests of the public. The only case of intrusion upon the privacy of a

17

County Gentleman . . . is one which the Promoters of the Bill venture to assert does not justify that opposition. Within the last twenty years the Gentleman alluded to, built, at a place called Styford on the north bank of the River Tyne, a modern dwelling-house. In selecting the site he did not show any great desire for seclusion, for the house is placed within 150 yards of a common highway . . . At that time he had no land on the opposite side of the river and if the Railway had been executed at any time previous to 1820, no part of his land would have been reached by it, but in 1823 he completed the purchase of a farm on the opposite side of the river. Through part of this farm, at a distance at the very nearest point of a quarter of a mile from his house and separated from it by a broad and rapid river, the Railway must necessarily pass. The Directors have taken every means in their power to satisfy this Gentleman; they have in vain urged that the passage of Railway carriages drawn by horses upon a level plain, unaccompanied by dust or noise, could occasion no annoyance to be compared with that of a common highway. They have asked if they could pass through his Estate in any way that would be more agreeable. The answer was "NO". They offered to raise a bank of earth and plant it with ornamental trees so as to exclude the carriages on the Railway entirely from the view of the house and grounds but all without avail, and the negotiation was finally closed by a formal communication from him "That no proposal the Directors of the Railway could possibly make to him would ever obtain his consent to the line passing along any part of his property".

Mr Bacon's attitude was contrasted unfavourably against that of other important people:

The line of Railway passes through the ornamental grounds of Corby Castle, the beautiful mansion of Henry Howard, Esquire, and yet that gentleman has the candour to concur in the judgment which so fixes the line, and the public spirit to aid its execution by becoming a Shareholder and by the execution of great zeal and talent in the performance of the duties of a Director of the Company. The line too, passes directly in front of Bywell Hall, the seat of Thomas Wentworth Beaumont, Esquire, MP, and nearer to it by one half the distance than to the house at Styford. Mr Beaumont too has the river intervening between his house and the Railway, but Mr Beaumont's name is not to be found amongst the Opposers of the Undertaking but in the list of subscribers to it.

18

Mr Bacon was depicted as a selfish landowner depriving the public of a great benefit. He was, of course, to oppose the Bill in Parliament.

At this time, the Newcastle–Carlisle road was covered with carts, day and night, taking about three days to do 60 miles. Two stage coaches, the *True Briton* and *Royal Mail*, ran daily, taking $8\frac{1}{2}$ hours for the journey. The railway was a necessity, and its supporters far outnumbered its opponents.

And so to the Bill in Parliament in 1829.

The Bill

Benjamin Thompson had the task of guiding the N & CR Bill through Parliament from 26 February 1829, and he faced 16 days of cross-examination in the Commons and 15 days in the Lords. He was assisted by six witnesses. Opposing him were 18 people, including the engineers Robert Stephenson, Joseph Locke and John Dixon (this last being resident engineer of the Liverpool & Manchester Railway). The Parliamentary evidence on the Bill extended to 329 closely-printed pages.

The main attack by the opposition was made in respect to the course of the N & CR, especially at places near to the Tyne and South Tyne which was subject to occasional flooding. George Leather, for example, drew attention to Thompson's proposed line at Hagg Bank, Wylam, where the 1828 flood of the Tyne had reached a level up to 5ft 0in above the proposed line. Thompson himself admitted that in an "ordinary flood" 10 miles, and in a "severe flood" 15 miles of the N & CR might be under water for up to 12 hours. Joseph Locke said that the level of the line should be raised. The South Tyne bridge at Warden would be several feet below the flood level. Robert Stephenson criticised the $1\frac{1}{2}$:1 slopes of the embankments and cuttings as being unsafe in wet weather. Part of Stephenson's cross-examination by Mr Adams for the N & CR, quoted by J. S. Maclean in his book *The Newcastle & Carlisle Railway*, is given below:

Adams: "Did you examine the nature of the soil?"

Stephenson: "I did in some places."

A: "In how many?"

S: "I examined it at Wylam Scars, at Eltringham Scars, at Riding Burn, and at Farnley Scars."

A: "You state that at Farnley Scars Mr Thompson's allowance for the slopes is not sufficient; did you look yourself at that part of the bank that lies near the river?"

S: "Yes, I know the bank perfectly."

A: "Is that $1\frac{1}{2}$ to 1?"

S: "No."

A: "That is nearly perpendicular."

S: "Yes."

A: "Does not that stand?"

S: "No, it is falling every day."

A: "How often have you been there to see that it is falling every day?"

S: "I heard that it was so."

A: "I desire to know whether that is not standing in a natural state."

S: "I will admit that it is perhaps 1 to 1."

A: "Is it not standing?"

S: "It was giving way."

A: "Will you undertake to say that it was giving way to any degree that is the least material?"

S: "I say that if an excavation was made through the hill it would give way."

A: "What is the nature of the soil at Farnley Scars?"

S: "It is a loose gravel mixed with clay. I give that opinion from report."

After much discussion on such matters, the Bill was read a second time on 6 March, and on 4 April the Commons adopted its preamble and several of its clauses by a 16:2 majority. The Bill received its third reading on 1 May. Shortly afterwards, Charles Bacon, who had of course opposed the Bill actively, saw that the N & CR was heading for success and decided to come to terms with the promoters. He agreed to offer no further opposition to the Bill and to let the company have seven acres of his land for the line, for £3,000, and with no necessity of raising a bank of earth to screen the line from Styford. Further, the N & CR was to prevail upon Mr J. Wilson to dispose of a portion of a hill intersected by the line, to his son Captain Bacon Grey. The N & CR Bill passed safely through the Lords during May, and received the Royal Assent—22 May 1829 (*10 Geo IV c 72*).

Early Construction Work

With the Act obtained, the company prepared to build its cross-country line. Francis Giles was employed as chief engineer for the line, and the company decided the first priority was to link Carlisle to the navigable Tyne at Blaydon. There was in fact some doubt about the course of the line at its east end—whether it should run from Newcastle to Lemington and Newburn and across the Tyne there, or follow Thompson's plan, and cross the river at Scotswood. As it happened, Giles favoured the Lemington route, but the company did not.

Construction commenced at both ends of the line in 1830–1, from Carlisle eastwards, and from Blaydon westwards. The gauge of the line was to be 4ft 8½in, while wrought-iron rails in 15ft 0in lengths weighing 42lb/yd laid on stone blocks comprised the permanent way. The very first work included the erection of the large viaducts at Wetheral and Corby, the Wetheral viaduct across the River Eden, and the Corby viaduct just to the east across the Corby Burn. The work on the former began on 25 March 1830, and both bridges, of handsome reddish sandstone, used stone from Cumbrian quarries. Wetheral viaduct was to have five arches of 80ft 0in span, reaching 95ft 0in above the Eden. The piers were 16ft 0in thick, and the length of the bridge was 564ft 0in. Corby bridge had seven arches of 40ft 0in span, reaching 70ft 0in in height, and was 480ft 0in long. Both viaducts had 22ft 0in width between parapets to allow a double line of rails; the N & CR intended to have its whole line as double track. There were also other important engineering activities at this end of the line, particularly the deep Wetheral, Cowran and Hell Beck cuttings, and the 73ft 0in high Hell Beck embankment. These works will shortly be mentioned in more detail; they entailed enormous expense, far more so than the overall relatively easy construction at the eastern end near Blaydon. The western section also included the heaviest gradient on the line—1 in 107 for some four miles between Wetheral and Milton, near Brampton, co-incident with the heaviest earthworks—both penalties for keeping the line to the south of both Hayton village and the town of Brampton.

The construction work was done by men and horses, and no steam locomotives were used at all. A typical newspaper advertisement by the N & CR reads as follows (from the *Newcastle Chronicle*, 14 August 1830):

> Newcastle-upon-Tyne and Carlisle Railway. Earthworkers who are wishing to enter into Contracts for executing Excavations and Embankments at the Western End of the Railway, are requested to send their Tenders for the same on or before the 17th of August next, to Messrs Hodgson & Nanson, Solicitors, Carlisle, at whose office Specifications and Sections are to be seen, and who will appoint a Person to show the Ground.

And on 2 October 1830:

> To Masons and Earthworkers: to be let in One Contract. The building a River Wall at Wylam Scars and forming the Roadway at that Place. Also, in 4 several contracts, the Excavation and Embanking several districts of the Line of Railway between Blaydon and Corbridge. To Iron Masters: the Directors of this Railway are willing to contract for the supply of 300 tons of Wrought Iron Rails and 90 tons of Cast Iron Chairs. The weight of the Rails to be 40 lbs to the yard. To Waggon-Wrights: A quantity of Waggons are wanted. Apply at the Railway Office, 16 Newgate Street, Newcastle.

At the same time money was required. On 21 August 1830 this notice was issued:

> Notice is hereby given that a CALL of £5 per share in the Newcastle and Carlisle Railway Company was made by the Directors of the said Company at a Meeting held this 16th Day of August 1830, and the Directors do direct and appoint that the Monies payable under, and by virtue of such Call, shall be paid to Robert Boyd, Esq., the Treasurer of the said company, at the Bank of Sir Matthew White Ridley, Bart, & Co. in Newcastle-upon-Tyne, on or

before the 16th Day of October next, and Notice is also hereby given that Shareholders who do not make payment of the above call previous to or on the 16th Day of October, will be charged interest at 5% from that Day, until the Amount shall be paid. James Losh, Chairman, 16th August 1830.

Work thus began and progressed during 1830–1, and the winter of 1831–2 was mild, allowing good progress. By late 1831 work at the eastern end had reached the Corbridge district. On 16 July the company called for tenders for the "excavating, embanking, draining and forming the Line of Railway from Dilston Water to Hexham", and the masonry work, sleepers, gates and fencing for this section. On 8 October the tenders were invited for "the making of a tunnel at Farnley Scars, 22 feet wide and from 200 to 300 yards long. Also, in one other lot, the making at Farnley Scars from 1 to $1\frac{1}{2}$ million of Bricks."

Ready capital was not always to hand. During 1832 the lack of money caused suspension of all work on the line, and a new Act of Parliament was hastily obtained on 23 June "to accelerate the raising by the Newcastle-upon-Tyne & Carlisle Railway Company of a certain sum for the more speedy prosecution of the undertaking", allowing £100,000 by loans. A third of this was at once borrowed from the Exchequer Loan Board, and work resumed. The rest of this sum came from the same source, all requiring repayment when traffic on the line began.

On 27 March 1833 Francis Giles reported to the annual meeting of the directors on progress with the line. He stated that work had been going on between Carlisle and Blenkinsopp (near Greenhead) and Stella (Blaydon) to Hexham. Thirteen miles of single line were formed between Stella and Hexham ready to take the stone blocks and rails; the other five miles at this end were not yet ready. At the western end, ten miles had been formed and another ten miles were being formed ready for the rails. A sum of £79,285 9s 2d (£79,285.46) had been paid to the contractors for all this work, and £14,231 15s 9d (£14,231.79) for iron bars, wagons and sleepers. The costs for land and damages were £18,032 10s 8d (£18,032.53). Of individual works, 30yd of Farnley tunnel at Farnley Scars, Corbridge, was ready (the length was to be 170yd), but difficulties were being found with the Wetheral and Cowran cuttings. A tunnel had been envisaged at the latter place but the nature of the sandy soil and the number of springs had ruled it out, and a deep cutting was the result. It was hoped to have some of the line open by the end of 1833, but this was not to happen. During 1833, Francis Giles was appointed to engineer the London & Southampton Railway, and agreed to remain consultant for the N & CR. His place was then taken by John Blackmore, who worked under a new "joint managing committee" of Messrs Benjamin Thompson, Nicholas Wood and George Johnson; this arrangement began from 25 June. In retrospect the loss of Giles was not important, for Blackmore was probably abler, and the committee equally talented.

Contracts for wrought iron-rails etc had been placed with two South Wales iron companies. They were to supply 6000 tons of rails at £5 0s 0d per ton and a corresponding number of chairs at £6 4s 0d (£6.20) per ton; also iron keys at £10 0s 0d per ton. All were to be delivered in 12 equal lots of 500 tons (rails) every two months after 1 May 1833, at Newcastle quay and Carlisle Canal Basin. The iron keys (ties) were to be laid at 10yd intervals to keep the rails in correct gauge.

The attractive Wetheral viaduct was completed by its contractor, William Denton, on 12 August 1834. The cost of its 350,000cu ft of stone had been £17,500. Cowran Hills cutting was the largest on the whole line and a considerable achievement, being probably the largest railway cutting in England in 1834. It was a mile long, quite straight for most of its distance, and reached 110ft 0in depth, being 90ft 0in—100ft 0in deep for 500yd. Its width varied from 26ft 0in at rail level, to 305ft 0in at the highest points, with the 1½:1 slopes terminated by 14ft 0in stone retaining walling at each foot. The Hell Beck cutting was less impressive, but reached 40ft 0in depth and was ¼-mile long. To the east was the Hell Beck embankment over the Hell Beck stream, which went through the embankment in a culvert. The embankment reached 73ft 0in at its maximum. A very handsome stone bridge lay between the Cowran and Hell Beck cuttings. This was a three-arch red sandstone structure crossing the river Gelt at an angle of 63°, reaching 64ft 0in above the Gelt. Each of the spans was 30ft 0in. This skew bridge was then the largest of its kind in Britain. Wetheral cutting was immediately east of the Eden bridge, and was ½-mile long and perhaps 60ft 0in deep.

At the eastern end, the stone-built Wylam Scars river wall was ¾-mile long, 26ft 0in above Tyne low-water level. To the west was a short cutting through Hagg bank, and a 1¼-mile low embankment (9ft 0in high) to Prudhoe. There was a deep cutting ¾-mile long east of Riding Mill, a single-span stone bridge over the Riding and Stocksfield burns. A wider bridge crossed the Devil's Water in one span, at Dilston. There were no heavy gradients in this section; the steepest slope was only 1 in 317 west of Prudhoe, to Stocksfield.

At the end of 1834 goods traffic was being operated between Blaydon and Stocksfield, using horse haulage. But the directors, particularly Nicholas Wood of the joint committee, had decided locomotives were necessary as horses would not make for speed, convenience, or efficient traffic operation. Therefore steam locomotives were ordered in November 1834, and the directors intended to apply to Parliament at an early date to rescind the clause in the 1829 Act prohibiting the use of locomotives on the line. This was to lead to more landowner trouble—with the Greys of Styford in particular—very soon.

At the end of 1834, the whole of the Blaydon—Hexham section was ready for use, although 12 miles were laid temporarily as a single line. By the end of the year over 115 tons of lead had been carried for T. W. Beaumont's lead company from Stocksfield to Blaydon (lead smelter) and another 491½ tons from Hexham to Blaydon, in horse-drawn wagons.

By March 1835, the first two locomotives had arrived and were in use. Both cost £1,053; No 2 *Comet*, built by R. & W. Hawthorns with 4-coupled wheels, was the first to arrive. No 1 *Rapid*, built by Robert Stephenson & Co, was delivered on 8

March, and was 6-coupled. Both had 12in × 16in cylinders, but *Comet* had a boiler pressure of 60lb/sq in and *Rapid* a 50lb/sq in boiler. They were painted red.

The First Opening, 9 March 1835

Passenger traffic began on 9 March 1835 with a ceremonial opening, the first such ceremonial occasion of several in the following few years. From 8.00 am on the day, crowds began making their way from Newcastle and Gateshead to Blaydon, where at the station *Rapid* and *Comet* were the chief attraction "on account of their construction and the beauty of their appearance". Carriages were attached to each locomotive, and open wagons with plank ("stout fir") seats were also added. The end result was two trains of 29 vehicles each. The weather was exceptionally fine, and a brass band played on the platform. Two other brass bands were in attendance—one travelling in each train. The late arrival of the Mayor of Newcastle and his party by river "state barge" delayed the planned 10.00am start of the procession, but at 10.45am *Rapid* took out its train for Hexham. *Comet* left at 10.54am and its progress was delayed by some of the open wagons ("cars") leaving the rails. Benjamin Thompson was a passenger in this second train. *Comet* had to replenish its water supply twice en route, from the river at Eltringham and near Farnley, because it had blown-off much steam awaiting the start. Hexham was duly reached, and at 3.20pm the return procession began. The Abbey bells sounded and various public demonstrations were made. Both trains, led by *Rapid*, reached Blaydon again in 70 minutes.

In the evening the Mayor of Newcastle, J. L. Hood, presided at a dinner in Newcastle Assembly Rooms. All the N & CR directors, promoters, many shareholders, etc, were present. The Mayor said he felt that they were justified in expecting a reasonably good return on their capital in comparison with the other two great railways, the Stockton & Darlington and Liverpool & Manchester. "When the N & CR was completed, the benefit to this part of the country would be astonishing, for it abounded in coal mines, the product from which would be carried by the railway." Matthew Plummer, N & CR chairman, proposed the health of the Duke of Northumberland and other landowners, and thanked them for assenting to the use of locomotive power without which they would not have dared to act in the "lawless" manner they had shown, without the consent of Parliament.

Benjamin Thompson spoke of the great credit due to Giles and Blackmore for the excellence of the construction work. No part of the line had had to be done a second time, and the works were standing well; the masonry work was substantial and the slopes well consolidated.

John Blackmore said that the work had not taken an unduly long time to construct. The cost per mile had been considerably less than the other lines of the same kind. The S & D and Leeds & Selby cost twice the N & CR—the Liverpool & Manchester cost four times as much.

The regular passenger service begun on 10 March had trains leaving Blaydon and Hexham at 8.00am, 11.00am, 2.00pm and 5.00pm. On Sundays, the only passenger trains left Blaydon at 8.00am and Hexham at 5.00pm. Newcastle passengers were conveyed to and from Blaydon by omnibus, or by steam boat from Newcastle quay when the tide was favourable.

The N & CR intermediate stations were at Ryton, Wylam, Prudhoe, Mickley, Stocksfield, Riding Mill and Corbridge. Station buildings were mainly of wood, the station houses of sandstone.

Bacon Grey's Intervention

Captain Bacon Grey of Styford, son of Charles Bacon, objected to the use of locomotives by the N & CR and he obtained an injunction to prevent their use. As a result the N & CR withdrew all services on 28 March 1835. An immediate public outcry resulted, and Bacon Grey saw the extent of the local feeling. After a while he gave in to public opinion, and the N & CR sounded all landowners on their views on steam locomotives. It was proposed to repeal the prohibiting clause of the 1829 Act. Opposition was little, provided that coke was used to make less smoke than coal, and on 6 May services resumed. On 17 June an Act was passed to legalise the use of locomotives.

Progress in 1836

A report on progress on 23 March 1836 stated that after a year's work, the earthwork and masonry work on the Hexham–Haydon Bridge section of the line was nearly finished, and the rails were being laid. The bridge over the river South Tyne at Warden, two miles west of Hexham, was nearly ready. River walling at Allerwash, where the line was close to the river, was completed. The station house and yard at Haydon Bridge were being prepared. "This section would have been practically finished by now except for very unfavourable weather during the last three or four months—frequent rains had so raised the river level that the masonry could not be proceeded with for weeks at a time.

Meanwhile, two more locomotives had appeared on the N & CR. These were No 3 *Meteor*, 4-coupled, built by E. Bury for £940 15s 0d and delivered on 7 September 1835. No 4 *Hercules* was 4-coupled, and delivered on 15 January 1836. It was built by Robert Stephenson & Co and cost £1,183 5s 4d. In May 1836 No 5 *Samson*, a 4-coupled machine by R & W Hawthorn, arrived, having cost £1,270. Another two Hawthorn locomotives were on order, with two more by Robert Stephenson. These had all been delivered by the end of 1836. The Hawthorns were No 6 *Goliath* (6-coupled) and No 8 *Tyne* (4-coupled). The Stephenson locomotives were No 7 *Atlas* (6-coupled) and No 9 *Eden* (4-coupled). *Goliath* and *Atlas* cost £1,420 each, *Tyne* £1,430, and *Eden* £1,484 15s 10d. *Eden* had a boiler pressure of 80lb/sq in, probably greater than any previous N & CR locomotive.

The western end of the line was in an advanced state by March 1836. Only three miles required laying with rails west of Blenkinsopp, and the rest was ready except for the cuttings near the Gelt bridge and at Wetheral. The London Road–Canal Basin section in Carlisle was in a "fairly forward state". Surveying was going on on the Blenkinsopp–Haydon Bridge section.

On 28 June 1836 the Hexham–Haydon Bridge section was officially opened to traffic. In particular this meant that the heavy lead traffic from the Allendale and Alston regions had a more convenient railhead at Haydon Bridge than previously. The main feature of the line was Warden Bridge designed by Blackmore. This had three stone piers with 50ft wooden truss spans and wooden platforms. (It was to be burned down in 1848—possibly by a spark—and rebuilt in cast iron on the old piers.) Intermediate stations were Warden and Fourstones.

Two special opening trains with the new locomotives *Samson* and *Hercules* were assembled at Blaydon. *Hercules* hauled five coaches and twelve open wagons with seats, while *Samson* had six carriages and eleven wagons. There were also several private carriages on each train. The trains left at about 11.00am, containing directors and guests, and reached Haydon Bridge just before 2.00pm. En route, Benjamin Thompson and friends joined at Wylam, and at Dilston crossing Mr Grey (Receiver of Greenwich Hospital) joined, and the flag of the hospital (which owned much land around Haydon Bridge) was hoisted onto one of the carriages. At Haydon Bridge a "triumphal arch of evergreens" was erected. The 1500 or so passengers returned to their trains at 4.30pm, reaching Blaydon at 6.30pm.

The western part of the line was then opened on 19 July 1836. Just before this, the Earl of Carlisle's re-aligned waggonway at Brampton had opened on 13 July. The waggonway had been re-aligned between Kirkhouse and Brampton coal staith to connect with the new N & CR at the planned Milton station, west of its old route. The N & CR lent a carriage (named *Emerald*) to the Earl for the opening of the re-routed line. The N & CR locomotive *Atlas* and the Earl's *Gilsland* also performed at the opening. The carriage *Emerald* also took part in the opening of the 28 miles or so of the N & CR from Carlisle to Blenkinsopp colliery.

To be ready for this opening, a few days before 19 July five loco-motives were sent by road from Haydon Bridge to Greenhead, but of these only *Hercules*, *Samson* and *Atlas* were ready for use. Also *Gilsland*, the Earl of Carlisle's locomotive, was borrowed for the ceremony.

At the opening, there were four trains which left a temporary station at London Road, Carlisle, for Blenkinsopp. *Samson* and *Hercules* pulled 17 vehicles each, *Atlas* had nine, and *Gilsland* five carriages. Covered carriages were as far as possible reserved for ladies. *Gilsland* was not in good condition and steamed badly, and the other trains had to wait for 45 minutes for it to catch up. The procession, with its 420 passengers, returned from Greenhead at 4.00pm. *Gilsland* failed on the journey, and *Hercules* broke a coupling near Scotby, leaving the Mayor and Corporation of Carlisle stranded for some time, until their plight was noticed.

Stations opened on the western section were at Carlisle (Rome Street temporary terminus), Scotby, Wetheral, How Mill, Milton, Low Row, Rose Hill (Gilsland), and Greenhead. A private halt at Naworth was established for the Earl of Carlisle at Naworth Castle. There was also, possibly, a private halt at Brampton Fell. The Blenkinsopp colliery terminus was of course temporary. The colliery itself at once sent coal traffic westwards to Carlisle. The various engineering features on this section, especially the grand Cowran Hills cutting (nearly one million cu yd of sand and clay removed), the Hell Beck cutting and em-bankment, and the Eden, Corby and Gelt bridges, attracted much notice. The Eden bridge had a footpath along its northern side. Henry Brooke wrote at this time:

> The cut through the Cowran Hills surpasses every other achieve-ment on the line. At first sight it is like an immense street, being as straight as an arrow, and it terminates by a viaduct which in the dis-tance has the appearance of a triumphal arch. So urgent was the necessity for its completion with its walls on each side that day and night in all weathers the men were kept working at it, the cutting being lighted up by naphtha lamps, and a fresh set of men going on

every 8 hours. The springs were diverted into a channel running along the centre of the railroad beneath the surface and providing a constant supply of fresh water for the inhabitants of Wetheral. The bridge over the Gelt woods is built in a graceful curve over some of the richest scenery in England.

A bridge across the river Petteril, near Carlisle, had three spans of 30ft 0in arching in ashlar. The passenger service on both Blaydon–Haydon Bridge and Blenkinsopp–Carlisle sections was co-ordinated, so that the gap between was covered by horse-drawn coaches on the road, connecting with trains on each section. Work had now begun in earnest to complete the missing link. The locomotives were based at Blaydon, Hexham, Haydon Bridge and Carlisle.

The Redheugh Branch

During June 1836, the N & CR had opened a length of line, $1\frac{1}{2}$ miles long, from Blaydon to Derwenthaugh, along the south bank of the Tyne. This utilised the route of the Blaydon, Gateshead & Hebburn Railway scheme (Act: 22 May 1834), the Blaydon company having run out of ready capital after building part of the Blaydon–Derwenthaugh section. The N & CR arranged with the BG & H that it, the N & CR, would build the line as far east as Redheugh, near Gateshead, and the BG & H could complete the rest to Hebburn. This route along the south side of the Tyne led the N & CR to re-consider its approach into Newcastle. Blackmore decided that a railway bridge over the Tyne at Redheugh was feasible, although it would be expensive. The BG & H liked this idea and a third railway, the Great North of England Railway which was planning a York—Newcastle line, also supported this plan. The Redheugh bridge plan was in fact arranged by the end of 1834. The Derwenthaugh–Redheugh section of the N & CR Redheugh branch was opened on 1 March 1837. The whole line had easy gradients, beside the river Tyne, and wooden bridges over the rivers Derwent and Team. Locomotive No 3 *Meteor*, the cheapest in stock in terms of

31

cost, was sent to work the Redheugh line service between Blaydon and Redheugh quay stations, with an intermediate station at Derwenthaugh. Passengers and goods were ferried across the Tyne from Redheugh to Newcastle, and a temporary station building at "The Close" was opened in Newcastle. However, many passengers continued to leave N & CR trains at Blaydon and go by boat or coach to Newcastle, which was as quick as going to Redheugh. The Redheugh service worked by *Meteor* was regarded as a branch service from the first; indeed, by 1837 the Redheugh bridge scheme was shelved on grounds of cost. Blackmore resurrected the Scotswood bridge scheme, to be started as soon as the Haydon Bridge–Blenkinsopp line was opened. The BG & H scheme collapsed, the Brandling Junction Railway being promoted instead to link Gateshead with Sunderland and South Shields.

1837–8

The N & CR managing committee report by Messrs Thompson, Johnson, and Nicholas Wood of 27 March 1837 said that work was under way west of Haydon Bridge. Good progress had been made with the long cutting towards Whitchester, east of Haltwhistle, and 200,000 cu yd of spoil from there would be used to form the 1-mile embankment beyond Haltwhistle. A change had been made in the course of the line at Ridley. Instead of following the Parliamentary course on the north bank of the South Tyne there, it was intended to carry the line more directly by means of two bridges over the South Tyne, which would save nine chains in distance, two crossings of the turnpike road, and some river walling. The re-aligned route would need a third river bridge— over the river Allen near Ridley, between the Tyne bridges.

At Carlisle, one shipping berth at the Canal Basin had been completed, and three others set out "to be finished when coal companies required them". The Canal Branch was opened on 9 March 1837 from Rome Street to the canal basin, where a new station replaced the temporary Rome Street structure. Although

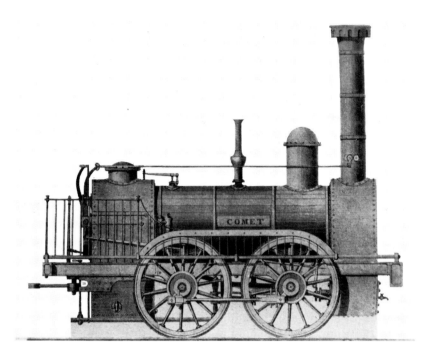

Old Newcastle & Carlisle Locomotives. *Above*: N&CR 0–4–0 No 2 *Comet*, of 1835. (*Ian Allan*). *Below*: NER 0–6–0 No 488, ex-N&CR No 40 *Langley*. (*Ian Allan*).

Carlisle. *Above*: Class 1440 2–4–0 No 1443 leaves Carlisle around the turn of the century on a slow train to Newcastle. This class was introduced in 1877. (*Real Photographs*). *Below*: Thompson LNER Class B1 4–6–0 No 1100 leaves Carlisle for Newcastle soon after World War II. (*Real Photographs*).

the canal basin was excellent for goods traffic it was not convenient for passengers to or from Carlisle, so a passenger station of a permanent nature was established at London Road, on the south-eastern side of the city. It was far from being an ideal station in some respects; it had no platforms although two lines were under a roof. Nearby the N & CR established its Carlisle locomotive depot and carriage sheds, later to be much improved.

More new locomotives were delivered to the company during 1837. No 10 *Lightning* arrived in January from Messrs Thompson; it cost £1,430 and was 4-coupled. Thompson's also built No 12 *Carlisle*, also 4-coupled, but only costing £1,405 and arriving on 9 June 1837. No 11 *Newcastle* was 6-coupled, cost £1,600, and arrived from Hawthorn in May. Further locomotives were on order for the completion of the "gap" in the line, during 1838. This opening, on 18 June 1838 from Blenkinsopp colliery, Greenhead, to Haydon Bridge, virtually completed the line across the narrowest neck of England. The event was duly celebrated at great extent, as will be related. Delivered to the N & CR in time for this were Hawthorn locomotives Nos 13 *Wellington* and 15 *Nelson* (costing £1,670 and £1,640), and Thompson's No 14 *Victoria* (£1,640). All were 4-coupled, and with 80lb/sq in boilers. Two further 4-coupled Hawthorns, Nos 16 *Northumberland* and 17 *Cumberland*, costing £1,670 each, came in October 1838. Coke ovens were erected at Derwenthaugh by the company to produce its locomotive fuel; surplus coke was sold.

During the first half of 1838 the "gap" was duly completed without delay. Timber bridges were erected over the South Tyne at Lipwood and Ridley, and over the Allen. Whitchester tunnel, east of Haltwhistle, was 202yd long, and straight; nearby the line had a length of river walling at the foot of an incised meander of the river. The line was never more than a mile from the South Tyne all the way west to Haltwhistle. Stations were built at Haltwhistle and Bardon Mill.

The "Gap" Completed—18 June 1838

The ceremonial opening was fixed for Waterloo day, 18 June, and on 15 June the directors and others went in a train over the whole line to see if all was ready. At 6.00am on 18 June, five trains left Carlisle, headed in order, by the *Eden, Goliath, Atlas, Samson* and *Hercules.* At 9.30am the firing of guns marked the arrival of *Eden* and its train at Redheugh. The Mayor and Corporation of Carlisle were in this train with some directors. The Mayor of Newcastle had the state barges ready, and these guests were all taken across the Tyne to the N & CR offices at The Close, and then to the Assembly Rooms in Westgate Road for breakfast. Train No 2 meanwhile decanted its passengers at Redheugh, and in haste they rushed up the gangway to a steam packet to convey them across the river. The gangway collapsed and 12 people or more had a morning bath in 3–4ft of coaly Tyne water. The rest of the arrivals went more smoothly. The trains were then re-arranged ready to leave for Carlisle at 11.00am. As usual, this hour passed with the main body of guests absent, and at noon the more distinguished guests and the directors arrived at Redheugh to find the carriages all occupied by the Gateshead corporation contingent and others less distinguished. The Mayor of Newcastle, and Matthew Plummer, N & CR chairman, for instance, had to find plank seats in an open "car". At 12.30 pm *Meteor* hauled out the first train. *Rapid* was pilot engine, with a Union Jack hoisted in front. *Meteor* had four carriages, and was followed by *Victoria* (nine carriages), *Wellington* (nine), *Nelson* (seven), *Lightning* (ten—including the Carlisle town band), *Tyne* (nine), *Carlisle* (eight), *Eden* (ten), *Goliath* (nineteen—with 600 passengers!), *Atlas* (seventeen, including Newcastle and Northumberland volunteers' band), *Samson* (eleven), *Newcastle* (nine), and *Hercules* (eight carriages). Only *Comet* was not in the procession. *Tyne*, incidentally, had a "steam organ" instead of a whistle, the organ invented by the Revd J. Birkett, vicar of Ovingham. At Blaydon, the locomotives took water, and thick fog then soon gave way to rain. Short stops were made at Corbridge, Hexham and Haydon Bridge, and the rain persisted as far as Milton. The last train reached the canal basin at 6.00pm, the average speed of the procession being 23mph. There were over 3,500 passengers.

The trains were re-marshalled to leave London Road station, while the guests looked at Carlisle and were refreshed in various ways. At 10.00pm the return began during a thunderstorm. "In the open carriages were hundreds of ladies who, in expectation of a sunny day and an early return, had come in light thin dresses without preparations for wet weather and a night journey." Their discomfiture in the heavy rain can be easily imagined. Near Milton station, *Carlisle* collided with the preceding train, derailing several carriages and *Carlisle*'s tender. Two passengers were injured, one having a broken rib. This event successfully delayed progress of most of the trains. It was 1.00am before the vehicles were re-railed and the journey could re-start, and all the while it rained heavily. The first train reached Redheugh at 3.00am, but the last one did not get there until after 6.00am. There had been a second collision at Greenhead in which an open wagon was damaged and two men severely hurt, one with a broken leg, the other a "mangled" arm. Thousands of people waited at Redheugh all night for the trains' return. By the morning, not only the bunting displayed all along the line was dishevelled!

Thus in 1838 the N & CR had completed its line across England, joining the navigable Carlisle Canal to the navigable River Tyne. It was not yet in Newcastle, but it was almost there, and steps were being taken to get there.

Some Personalities

A great number of people had co-operated to make the N & CR a reality. The chairman in 1838, Matthew Plummer, was just one of many, but he was an able leader in those early days. Born in 1771, he was to become a partner in a glassworks and a flax mill, a coal owner and property owner, on Tyneside. He was also

American vice-consul in Newcastle. He had helped the N & CR from 1825 monetarily and otherwise and became a director, assuming the chairmanship in 1833. He kept this office until 1848, guiding the company on its upward path to prosperity. As Maclean wrote: "His management did much to ensure the success of the N & CR."

Benjamin Thompson's role has been mentioned already. His route for the line was adopted for much of its course; he guided the Bill through Parliament, and became one of the three members of the joint managing committee. Before the N & CR days he had built many wagonways in the Tyneside area; he had been managing partner in a colliery company. He died in 1867.

James Losh (1763–1833) was another principal N & CR supporter. He was Recorder of Newcastle, becoming first chairman of the N & CR after its initial meeting. He and his brother William bought together £10,600 worth of shares in the company at the outset. James Losh, junior, became its chairman in July 1851.

William Woods (1787–1864) became the N & CR chairman in its latter days up to 1862. Again, he had been a principal promoter, and a director. He became a director of the North Eastern Railway after the amalgamation of 1862.

In the early years of the company, the list of directors was a distinguished one indeed. In 1835 they included the Earl of Durham, the Mayors of Newcastle and Carlisle, and Messrs T. W. Beaumont, MP, and Matthew Bell, MP. Benjamin Thompson was also a director. The Earl of Carlisle had a representative on the board, this being John Ramshay. The Earl held no shares but was himself eligible to be appointed a director if he chose, during the company's existence.

John Adamson was the N & CR secretary for much of the company's history, and his name appeared at the foot of the company's notices. Anthony Hall, locomotive superintendent, was a "character", who came from the Stockton & Darlington Railway. He appears to have been very popular with his men, and when he retired in September 1862 the directors presented him with a handsome tea service and a testimonial.

With a minor position, but not lost to history, was Thomas Edmondson. In 1836 at the age of 44, Edmondson joined the N & CR as a clerk at the new Milton station, at £60 per annum. He thought out a cardboard ticket system, and invented a dating press and racks for holding the stacked tickets in numerical order. The N & CR had, prior to Edmondson's ideas, a complicated book-keeping system at the principal stations, while at the minor stations passengers paid their fares to the stationmasters, who handed the money to the train guards. In August 1837 Edmondson built a hand printing press for tickets, and in 1838 printing machinery, which printed tickets from type while a train of four wheels automatically rotated, printing the consecutive numbers as the tickets emerged from the press. All this was confined to Milton station at first, but the ticket system was soon extended to other stations. It seems the N & CR was going to move Edmondson to its offices in Newcastle by 1839, but Captain Laws of the Manchester & Leeds Railway met him in March 1839 and offered him a position on that line at £120 a year. Edmondson accepted and left when the M & L opened in June. Later he tried to make use of his ideas in Manchester by opening a factory to produce ticket machines, presses and racks, to meet the increasing national demand.

CHAPTER 2

The N & C Railway Company

Some Features of Operation

An interesting feature of the N & CR was the running of trains on the right-hand line of double-track sections, ie the down trains (from the east) on double track ran on the northern track, the trains from the west running on the southern track. This was not unique, but it was not common on English railways. The single-track sections on the line in 1840 were Stocksfield–Hexham, and Rose Hill–Milton. At about 1840, some signals began to be used on the line. These consisted of revolving poles with red discs 4ft 0in in diameter with handles to turn them, the showing of the red disc being considered to block both lines, so that a train arriving at a station where another was standing on the other line had to wait for the first train to leave. This is a probable explanation for the number of stations with staggered platforms, notably Wylam and Haltwhistle; staggered platforms allowed both platforms to be occupied at the same time.

In 1841 Dr Granville, in his *Spas of England*, described quite a number of N & CR station houses as being "perfect specimens of taste and style in architecture", and indeed they were neat and attractive. Hexham station, one of the most important on the line, at first had no platforms, but soon acquired two and two bays or sidings, and a roof of four spans on light cast-iron columns covering three lines. In the early days a smithy and a stable adjoined Milton station buildings. In fact Tomlinson, who generally thought poorly of the standard of early stations in north-east England, managed to give some praise to the N & CR stations. Gordon Biddle, in *Victorian Stations* (David & Charles, 1973), also devoted some favourable attention to them. He called them "neat practical stations, at one with their surroundings", remarking that it was uncertain who designed them but suggesting the likelihood of Benjamin Green, who was only 26 years old in 1835. Mr Biddle's commentary is worth quoting:

All in ashlar with slated roofs, the most common platform buildings on this line were two-storeyed rectangular in plan, and embellished only with a cross-gabled corbelled-out centrepiece, as at Riding Mill, Greenhead, Gilsland (*originally Rose Hill*) and Brampton Junction (*originally Milton*), with Tudorish chimneys and moulded window hoods. Only superficially different were Wylam and Stocksfield, where the centrepiece was omitted. Little single-storey station houses were built to match, detached at Stocksfield, Haydon Bridge and Hexham, but forming part of the main building at Scotswood. The importance of Haltwhistle was recognised in a strong two-storey Tudor residence having large gables, Maltese-cross fashion, with smaller repeats and five clustered chimney shafts. Bardon Mill was somewhat similar but much smaller. The odd man out, Corbridge, was probably rebuilt in 1848, and was curiously like a private house with an added platform verandah on nice Tuscan columns. Wetheral also had the later addition of an iron-and-glass roof over the working area of the platform. Whishaw, ever the perfectionist, grumbled about some of the buildings, being set back too far from the rails, as they remained throughout their existence. At Hexham the light iron trainshed was detached from the station buildings, while at London Road, Carlisle, as much as 20 yards separated the Tudor office building from the wooden shed, leaving passengers to stumble over intervening tracks. At others, platforms were added, as time went on, and some even had glass roofs built over the objectionable open space, as at Gilsland, only to be removed again in more recent times.

The N & CR rolling stock appearance was bright and attractive. The bright red livery of the locomotives was not common in Britain. The names were picked out in bold letters upon a red background space on each boiler and tender side. In 1839 the N & CR stock comprised 21 locomotives, 12 first-class carriages, 6 mixed, 12 second-class, 220 four-wheeled goods wagons, 56 ballast wagons, 36 cattle wagons, 570 coal-coke chaldron wagons, 9 double sheep pens and some luggage vans with seats on top. The first-class carriages were painted yellow, lined black with a crown in the centre panel and the crests of arms of Newcastle and Carlisle respectively on the two outer compartment panels. Second-class carriages were black, lined in green, while luggage vans, horse boxes etc, were green. About 1843 claret became the standard passenger carriage colour. The N & CR passenger guards wore scarlet laced coats, drab coloured trousers and cream hats, a uniform similar to that worn by the guards on the old mail stage coaches which the railway superseded.

The N & CR was an innovator in tackling operational problems as they emerged. Snow was an obvious winter problem; the company is said to have tied two besoms to a locomotive on 21 October 1836 to sweep snow from the rails. In 1837 a man named William Hawthorn brought out his "railway engine protector" to clear obstacles on the rails, and in 1840 all the N & CR locomotives are believed to have been fitted with these small "ploughs" in front of the leading wheels. The N & CR is also credited with the first experiment with sanding apparatus, to check wheel-slipping by locomotives.

Snow was an annual problem for many railways. The N & CR reaching less than 500ft altitude was not to have the problem as frequent and disrupting as certain other British railways, although its branch to Alston, reaching a higher level in the Pennines, was occasionally to suffer badly. In March 1846, a "great snowstorm" affected the North-East. A report on 21 March stated that "westward Greenhead seems to have been the utmost limit as none was seen at Carlisle. Indeed beyond Hexham the snow was very trifling. This is proved by the fact that the trains on the Newcastle and Carlisle Railway coming eastward kept their time up to the Hexham station while between there and Newcastle, a loss of $3\frac{1}{4}$ hours occurred to the first train."

Locomotives 1839–41

When locomotive No 26 *Saturn* was delivered in April 1841 there was no further addition to the stock for over five years. Four had arrived in 1839, three from Hawthorns and one from Thompson Bros. At a cost of £1839, No 18 *Durham* was 6-coupled, had 90lb/sq in boiler pressure, and was the most powerful and most expensive locomotive then in stock. Nos 19 *Sun* and 20 *Star* both 0–4–2s, came in November 1839, and like *Durham* were from Hawthorns. They cost £1839 16s 0d each. No 21 *Matthew Plummer* was named after the chairman, and was 6-coupled, being built by Thompson for £1563 19s 0d. During April 1840 another Thompson 0–6–0, No 22 *Adelaide* arrived, and later in the year came No 23 *Mars* and No 24 *Jupiter*. No 25 *Venus* appeared on 18 January 1841 and was followed by No 26 *Saturn*, continuing the planet sequence. Nos 22–26 each cost £1650; some were 0–6–0s, others 0–4–2s. *Jupiter*, like *Durham*, had a 90lb/sq in boiler. *Adelaide* was the last to be bought with a 60lb/sq in boiler. All the locomotives from No 15 *Nelson* to No 26 *Saturn* had 14in × 18in cylinders, as did several of the earlier ones, such as *Hercules* and *Atlas*. 12 of the 26 locomotives were from R. & W. Hawthorn.

The Entry into Newcastle

The N & CR reached Newcastle in 1839. The three miles of line from Blaydon into Newcastle via Scotswood were constructed throughout 1838, including the bridge over the Tyne, designed by John Blackmore. Between Scotswood and the Shot Tower station, the line ran on a course close to the Tyne near the foot of the steep north bank of the river, and was embanked in places and partly in cuttings at others. On 21 May 1839 the line was opened with some ceremony, *Meteor* being brought from the Redheugh branch to haul the special train. Thereafter some goods traffic used the line, but it was not ready for passenger traffic. On 21 October it was at last opened for regular passenger

43

trains, but the wet weather of late had caused some landslips, and it was deemed necessary to close the line almost at once until 2 November, to repair the defects. Single-line working was in use for a short time, but double track was laid and soon both tracks were in use. The Newcastle station was close to "Parker's lead factory". By the end of 1839 the N & CR was for the first time running directly between the two towns in its title. The Redheugh branch service continued, and for goods, this line was much used because of the convenience of Redheugh quay on the Tyne. The N & CR carried much timber from Russia and Scandinavia, landed on the Tyne, and carried by rail to Carlisle, for trans-shipment to Liverpool or Ireland. The line thus formed a vital link between the North Sea and Irish Sea, especially before other railways reached Carlisle from the south, as they did in the 1840s.

The Scotswood railway bridge was $\frac{1}{4}$-mile west of the existing road suspension bridge. It crossed the Tyne at an oblique angle, and was wholly of timber, except for the abutments, consisting of a series of trussed ribs resting on ten piers, which were composed of piles braced together, the span of each opening being 60ft 0in measured on the skew line. It had 35ft 0in clearance above low water level. Needless to say wooden piers were not the best material to be long-lasting, and the bridge formed something of a hazard to river traffic.

The "Mania"——Ending of Isolation

The 1840s saw the N & CR cease to be an isolated line across the Tyne gap of England, when new railways were built and linked to it at both ends, Carlisle and Newcastle. The N & CR had itself planned a major branch from its line, aimed at Scotland, from near Hexham via the North Tyne valley to the Scottish Borders around Hawick. This came to nought, but is discussed separately later. There were also plans put into effect in 1845 for two branch lines, one of which, the Alston branch, succeeded, and this is also mentioned separately.

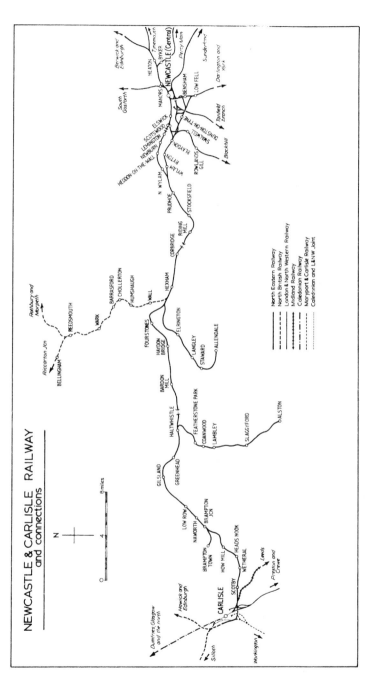

Fig 1 Map of Newcastle & Carlisle Railway and connections

At Carlisle, the most important new lines opened were the Lancaster & Carlisle Railway (opened December 1846), which provided a continuous line of rails from London to Carlisle, the Caledonian Railway (opened fully February 1848), continuing the west coast main line to Glasgow, and the locally important Maryport & Carlisle Railway (opened in May 1843), which virtually continued the N & CR to Maryport on the Cumberland coast, and with which company the N & CR had early, close relations. Indeed, the M & C used the N & CR London Road station for its passenger trains (at an annual charge of £250), and the opening of the Wigton–Carlisle section was celebrated with the N & CR locomotive *Star* and others, and N & CR carriages. John Blackmore himself was both N & CR and M & C chief engineer. The N & CR offered the Lancaster & Carlisle company similar facilities as the M & C at London Road, and the L & C used London Road until its own Carlisle "central" (ie Citadel) station—joint with the Caledonian—was opened. The L & C had a curve from Upperby to join the N & CR line facing east, necessitating reversal, to reach London Road. This curve remained after the Citadel station was opened, for through goods traffic.

At the eastern end of the N & CR, links were effected with new lines. On 15 January 1839 the Redheugh incline of the Brandling Junction Railway, from beside the river and joining the N & CR line at Redheugh, up a 1 in 23 gradient and rope haulage to Oakwellgate, opened; also the Brandling Junction main line from Gateshead to Sunderland, opened during 1839. The Redheugh incline thus provided a link between the N & CR and the lines to eastern Durham. More important was the opening of the Newcastle & Darlington Junction Railway from Darlington (joining the Great North of England Railway, from York) to Gateshead, opened in April 1844. The N & DJ had taken over the Brandling Junction company by the end of that year, and was actively preparing plans for a bridge across the Tyne to Newcastle. George Hudson, the Railway King, was also behind the Newcastle & Berwick Railway scheme of 1845, and foresaw the N & DJ and N & B lines using a joint central station in Newcastle. The N & CR was aware of this, and wished also to use such a central station, for the better interchange of traffic. Incidentally, the N & CR had a similar wish to use Carlisle Citadel station, but found its new neighbour, the Lancaster & Carlisle, not at all cooperative in this respect, mainly because the L & C demanded a somewhat exhorbitant charge for allowing the N & CR to use the station. The east coast lines were to be more sympathetic regarding Newcastle. It is an interesting point that the N & CR, the oldest of the lines at Carlisle and almost the oldest at Newcastle (Newcastle & North Shields Railway excepted), found acceptance when it wished to use Newcastle's central station with the newer east coast lines, but was spurned by its newer west coast neighbours at Carlisle. In consideration of later history, the N & CR, with its headquarters at Newcastle, was, from the beginning, more an "eastern" line than a "west coast" one. On the line, down trains were from Newcastle and not Carlisle, the up trains being from Carlisle. The west coast group, however, did make an attempt to get hold of the N & CR very early on.

Finance and Operations to 1850

The N & CR's income from traffic was usually at between £1700 and £2000 per week by early 1847. As an example the receipts for the week ending 16 January 1847 were:

Passengers	£553	18s	11d
Goods	£1485	11s	6d

Total revenue in 1847 was no less than £115,825 8s 1d (£115,825.40½). The company was thus in a reasonably healthy financial state, paying 6% in 1840, 5% in 1841 and 6% in 1847. In 1842 the ratio of expenditure to receipts on the line was 40%, just below the national average. The rates and fares charged were as reasonable as any at the time. In 1847, for example, the fares (single) from Newcastle (or Redheugh) to Carlisle were 11s

0d (55p) first-class, 8s 6d (42½p) second-class, and 5s 0d (25p) third-class. (Third-class was introduced early in 1847.) Children under 12 were charged half price. Parcels were charged 1s 0d (5p) if carried over 40 miles, provided they weighed below 42lb. "All parcels must be delivered at least 15 minutes before the time of starting, or they cannot go until the following train." Further, "The Company will not be accountable for loss of, or damage to any parcel for more than £5 unless registered, and insurance paid for it in proportion to its value".

Examples of goods and minerals charges at this time may be given. Coal and coke for landsale, carried in N & CR wagons, 1¾d per ton per mile for below 10 miles; coal for shipment, 1½d similarly. Figures for coal carried in private wagons were different: 1½d for landsale, 1⅛d for shipment. Lime was charged at 1d per ton per mile for over 24 miles, 1¼d for below 10 miles. Other commodities also were charged according to distance to be carried. Lead ore, 2½d per ton per mile for below 20 miles, 2d above that distance; cheese went at 3d above 40 miles but 4d below that distance; salt herrings went at 4d for below 20 miles, 3½d 20–40 miles and 3d above 40 miles; geese went any distance at 3d each; vitriol (acid) had the heavy charge of 6¾d for below 40 miles, 6d above 40 miles. The horse had a more complex system of rates as did cows, sheep and pigs; a horse carried for 55–60 miles was charged at no less than £1, but if under 20 miles, the charge was only 7s 6d (37½p). The company also informed those wishing to make use of its services, general conditions such as the following:

No smoking allowed in any of the Stations or Coaches even with the consent of the Passengers. The Doors of the Booking Offices will be closed 5 minutes before the time of starting, after which no Passenger can be admitted. No fees or Gratuities allowed to be taken by any servant of the Company. No Goods will be received at any of the Stations after 7 o'clock in the evening,—*and to cover everything generally*—The Company give Notice that they will not be answerable for any loss or Damage to any Goods in their hands as Carriers, or in their Warehouses, or upon their Landing Places arising from Fire, the Act of God or Civil Commotion; or to any Animals sent by their Trains, although every proper Precaution will be taken to Secure their Safe Conveyence. Glass uninsured, Furniture, all hazardous and brittle articles, are conveyed at the risk of the Owners.

In the 1840s the N & CR had a heavy traffic in coal, lead and timber, the Northern Pennines lead mining activities being at a very active level, whilst timber docked from Scandinavia and Russia on the Tyne was conveyed across country to Carlisle for movement to Lancashire and Ireland as earlier mentioned. It was the lead industry which caused the company to look at the prospect in 1844–5 of building a branch railway into the Pennines to the Alston district, so that the mines would have an easier access to Tyneside.

On the passenger side, the company ran many excursion trains, and the first on 13 April 1840 from Carlisle to Newcastle in connection with a "Polytechnic Exhibition" there is often considered to be the very first British excursion train, although earlier instances of cut fares exist. The fare was 10s 0d (50p) for a return to Carlisle, a 6s 0d (30p) reduction. Following the success of excursion trains, next step was the Sunday excursion, and this was by no means acceptable to many people of the time. There was a strong-rooted objection to any "abuse" of the Sabbath by many folk at this time, and the N & CR Sunday excursions were a bone of contention; in one case a director resigned over this matter because he thought such trains wrong. Thus Peter Dixon wrote to Chairman Matthew Plummer on 4 April 1846: "Another reason which has induced me to resign from the Direction is the continuance and frequency of the Cheap Sunday Trains; a practice against which I have always protested, but which I see no reason to hope will be speedily discontinued." At Company's meetings the Sabbatarians repeatedly pressed for a complete closure of the line on Sundays. The directors, they said, were violating the Scriptures and encouraging low moral standards, preventing their servants from enjoying a day of rest and finally providing transport for people who could easily travel on another day of the week. Nevertheless the general meeting of

March 1847 after much discussion rejected by a large majority a demand that the mail trains should be run without passenger coaches (see *The Opposition to Sunday Rail Services in NE England*, by D. Brooke). The opposition to all Sunday trains continued to the end of the company's existence. The excursions were many and varied, but places such as Hexham, Stocksfield, Milton (Naworth Castle) and Rose Hill (Gilsland Spa) were common attractions. The Sunday excursion from Newcastle to Carlisle on 29 August 1840 attracted the notice of the Revd W. C. Burns, a Scottish Sabbatarian, who reacted with handbills and placards condemning the whole operation:

> A reward for Sabbath breaking
> People taken safely and swiftly to Hell!
> Next Lord's Day, by the Carlisle Railway for 7s 6d.
> It is a Pleasure Trip!

However, one can possibly see the point of view of Sabbatarians at that time, with their straightforward view that the Holy Day was a Day of Rest.

On 17 March 1849 one Thomas H. Graham of Carlisle had the following notice "To the Shareholders of the Newcastle & Carlisle Railway" published in the *Newcastle Daily Journal*:

> Ladies and Gentlemen: I beg to inform you that I propose at the Annual Meeting of the Proprietors of the N & CR Company to be held at Newcastle on Tuesday the 27th inst., to renew the Motion I made last year for the Cessation of all work on the Lord's Day, except in cases of necessity and mercy. A Return made to Parliament of the Accidents on the Scottish Railways from January to June 1848, shows the comparative Security of Sabbath Observing and Sabbath Breaking lines. The Lines running Sabbath trains embraced 280 miles, the lines having no Sabbath trains embraced 240 miles. Upon the Lines which run Sabbath Trains within the period mentioned, 16 Accidents occurred; 14 persons were killed and 2 wounded; on the Lines that observed the Sabbath there were only 2 Accidents, 1 Person was killed and 1 wounded. Without asserting that these facts show a miraculous Divine interposition, I would confidently affirm that the Providence of God concurs with

Above: Gelt viaduct from the north. (*Author*). *Below*: NER Class D20 (R) 4–4–0 on an up train, Stocksfield. (*J. W. Armstrong*).

Stations – 1 *Above*: Haltwhistle station. (*Folk Train*). *Below*: NER Atlantic No 705 heads a Newcastle bound train at Haltwhistle. (*Real Photographs*).

the Law of God, and that when Men have not the rest of the Holy Sabbath, they become jaded and over-fatigued, and less equal both bodily and mentally for the discharge of their duties upon the other 6 days of the week.

On the subject of accidents, in August 1840 Oswald Gardener, driving a train at Stocksfield, was killed when the locomotive broke a connecting rod. His grave can be seen in Whickham churchyard.

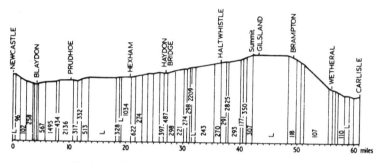

Fig 2 Gradient profile of Newcastle & Carlisle line

The company's locomotives, besides only burning coke, were fitted with sanding apparatus from 1838 to prevent slipping, and had "ploughs" in front of the leading wheels in case of meeting obstacles on the line, which was for long not fully fenced. Thomas Graham, driver of No 11 *Newcastle*, was fatally crushed when the locomotive and tender were derailed by a stray cow at Ryton in December 1844. There was a similar, but non-fatal event at Haydon Bridge on 29 November 1845. On 18 December 1847 the *Newcastle Journal* devoted a long paragraph to a railway accident:

An unfortunate accident occurred on Tuesday last to Mr T. O. Blackett, land surveyor of this town. He was on the line of the N & CR near Eltringham, when the $\frac{1}{4}$ to 2 o'clock train from Newcastle came up. The engine driver observing him, immediately blew his whistle but perceiving that no notice was taken of his warning, he was compelled in order to avoid an accident, to put off the steam.

Before, however, the train could be stopped, it approached the spot where the unfortunate gentleman was standing, who not perceiving it till it was close upon him, sprang to the side but, stumbling against some blocks, he fell with his left hand on the rails, and one of the carriages passed over it causing severe mutilation. Another engine was procured at Mickley Colliery, and a carriage being taken from the train, Mr Blackett was immediately conveyed to the Newcastle Infirmary, where it was found necessary to amputate the hand at the wrist. Though he received other injuries sanguine hopes of his recovery are entertained.

Another fatal accident, perhaps typical of any railway, is recorded in the *Newcastle Journal* of 12 January 1850:

An accident occurred upon the N & CR on Monday last at the Corbridge station, by which an old woman aged 70 years of the name of Ann Wailes came to her death. It appeared that the deceased who was a passenger alighting at the Corbridge station did not make that effort requisite to leave the train while stationary, but in attempting to do so after it was in motion, accidently fell between the carriages and the platform, by which one of her legs was so mutilated as to render amputation necessary and she died from the exhaustion consequent thereupon. An inquest was held and a verdict of accidental death returned.

There was not to be what could be called a really serious accident on the N & CR throughout its history, but minor accidents and injuries, such as those just mentioned, do seem to have been fairly common, but perhaps no more so than on other contemporary railways.

In 1846, the first new locomotives for five years arrived on the N & CR. No 27 *Globe* and No 28 *Planet* were 6-coupled, had 90lb/sq in boilers, and were built by Hawthorn for £2250 each. The next year two more Hawthorn locomotives, this time 4-coupled, arrived as No 29 *Albert* and No 30 *Swift*. Two 6-coupled locomotives came in September–October 1848, No 31 *Collingwood* and No 32 *Allen*. These had cylinders 16in × 24in, 85lb/sq in boiler pressure, and were Hawthorn Nos 669–70, costing £2300 each. Nothing came in 1849, but in 1850 Robert

Stephenson Nos 764–5 came, 6-coupled locomotives Nos 33 *Alston* and 34 *Hexham*, cylinders 15in × 22in, 90lb/sq in boilers, delivered on 17 June and 17 July respectively. These cost only £1770 each, which is well below the cost of all 1846–8 locomotives. Both of these were much later to be rebuilt by the NER, prolonging their active lives, as were many other N & CR engines.

On the line itself, the late 1840s saw preparations for the building of the Newcastle Central Station, designed by John Dobson. The N & CR was to be only a junior partner in Central Station, the York, Newcastle & Berwick Railway being the main occupant. A Newcastle & Berwick Railway (as it then was) advertisement of 23 January 1847 on the "Station at Newcastle" announced:

> to Railway contractors, Builders and others.—The Directors of this Railway are ready to receive Tenders for the Formation and Completion of the following works—the Building and Entire completion of the New Station in Neville Street, Newcastle. Plans, Sections, and Specifications of the Works may be seen and any Information obtained at the office of Mr. John Dobson, Architect, New-Bridge Street, Newcastle, on and after Monday the 25th of January, inst. Parties proposing to Tender for these Works are requested to meet on Tuesday the 26th of January at Mr Harrison's office in Newcastle at 12 o'clock, for the purpose of appointing Parties to take out the Quantities. (signed) George Hudson, *Chairman.*

In fact the Hudson affair was to delay the completion of Central Station, which eventually opened on 29 August 1850, Queen Victoria and Prince Albert officially declaring it open, although externally it was not complete. The magnificent colonnade, the main external feature, was missing, but was built and lasts to this day. N & CR passenger trains began to use the station regularly from 1 January 1851, Forth Banks remaining the goods station.

More mundanely, in December 1844 the N & CR called for tenders for building offices and a "shed" for the protection of the trains at Blaydon station. As one of the busiest stations, Blaydon needed reasonable facilities, which were provided. During 1844 the two sections of single-track line were doubled; traffic was not interrupted except when part of Farnley Tunnel, Corbridge, collapsed during the widening on 28 December 1844, affecting passage of this point for several days. In 1848 the wooden Warden Bridge was burned down. A temporary structure was erected whilst the old bridge was rebuilt, using cast-iron arched ribs resting on the old piers and abutments. The rebuilt bridge was to last till 1903.

Weather conditions only on occasion have affected the N & CR which, as it rises nowhere over 500ft above sea level, is usually spared long "Arctic" periods. But it has had its moments, as with the 1846 example mentioned earlier.

One of the company's most well-known claims to fame, was the card ticket, replacing its earlier paper efforts. The process of booking a passenger a paper ticket was a slow one, the clerk having to write in on ticket and counterfoil, its number, date and often other information, which was obviously difficult at busy periods. This was one reason for closing booking office doors some minutes before a train was due. At Milton station was Thomas Edmondson, who thought out the idea of printing and issuing cardboard tickets numbered consecutively. In August 1837 he invented a dating-press. In late 1838 Edmondson's system of printing and dating tickets was put into general use on the N & CR, greatly easing ticket issue, and the keeping of accounts at stations. The genius of Edmondson was noted by the Manchester & Leeds Railway who obtained his services in 1839 for £120 per annum (his salary at Milton had been £60), but the Edmondson system of tickets belongs to N & CR history.

The Hudson Interlude

George Hudson, the "Railway King", became for a relatively short time, shadowy overlord of the N & CR. His downfall did not, however, bring any serious financial damage to the N & CR, which retained its independence remarkably in this spell.

The basic fact in 1848 was that there were developing two

main lines of rail from London to Scotland, an east coast and a west coast route. The N & CR had to link with both at a strategic crossing of Northern England, so would be a useful cross-country feeder line for either route to control.

In 1845–7 the N & CR had cast acquisitive eyes on its western neighbour, the Maryport & Carlisle. This Cumbrian line was flourishing with mineral traffic, and could easily have become a western continuation of the N & CR. However, the M & C knew its own worth, and whilst it received the N & CR overtures it made it plain a union or a lease would cost the N & CR more than a little. The N & CR was unwilling to meet the M & C price and the N & CR directors' report of 28 March 1848 states the facts:

> The negotiations with the Maryport and Carlisle Co. for a perpetual lease to this Company of that Railway which was pursued for some time, has been terminated. The terms proposed by the M & C Rly. Co being such as could not be prudently entertained.

Perhaps a merger would have worked!

Also in March 1848, the N & CR itself received a proposal. The Caledonian Railway, linking Carlisle to Glasgow (opened in February), offered to lease the N & CR, and this was followed by another offer, the York, Newcastle, Berwick Railway also offering a lease. On 25 April 1848 the N & CR held a special meeting of the directors to consider these offers. The directors stated that "the offers made are not sufficiently advantageous to induce the Directors to recommend the acceptance of either of them to the Shareholders". (The Caledonian offered 6% dividend in perpetuity and all profits of up to 8%, or alternatively, 6% for five years, and 7% thereafter with no share in profits over 7%. The YNB offered 6% for 3 years, and 7% thereafter. The YNB itself paid a 9% dividend in 1847.) But on 31 May a shareholders' meeting, perhaps intoxicated with thoughts of huge dividend returns à la Hudson, decided "that the offer of Mr Hudson for a perpetual lease of the N & CR . . . be accepted". The directors could only now consent, and the leasing agreement was signed on

5 July, effective from 1 August 1848.

The YNB was also to lease the Maryport & Carlisle Railway, and to manage the two lines leased, as the Newcastle, Carlisle & Maryport Railway, although in practice little was affected combining the two lines. An Act was necessary to put the leasing into legality, and this was not done. However, from August the working arrangements with the Maryport line became closer, especially for through goods traffic. For passengers better timings were made for interchange between N & CR and M & C trains at Carlisle, omnibuses being provided to carry passengers between the stations there. (The Maryport & Carlisle had opened its own station in Bog Street.)

The N, C & MR manager was James Allport, who had little chance to make his mark, because by early 1849, rumblings of discontent with Mr Hudson were already occurring in the various railways he controlled. Even the YNB shareholders were not all happy with the Carlisle–Maryport leases, as their own company, so recently formed by amalgamations, was not cohesive after so short a time. During 1849 the Hudson drama was played out, he being held in national focus with allegations of illegal or irregular share and financial transactions, which were to ruin his career. The Bill for the YNB to lease the N & CR and M & C failed to become law, so from 1 January 1850 the two lines resumed their own independent operations. Mr James Allport went in 1850 to be general manager of the Manchester, Sheffield & Lincolnshire Railway, eventually becoming general manager, and then chairman of the Midland Railway, where he showed his great talents. Henry Smiles became N & CR Manager. Matthew Plummer, chairman up to 1848, was 79 years of age, and a new chairman was elected to succeed Mr Hudson in 1851. (Mr Plummer died in 1856.) James Losh (Vice-Chairman) who was the son of another James Losh, N & CR Chairman up to 1833, became Chairman. George Dixon of Carlisle became vice-chairman.

A last word on the period comes from the N & CR secretary's letter (John Adamson) to the Shareholders on 20 March 1850, stating that the Company:

> are glad to inform the Shareholders that they are proceeding satisfactorily to the settlement of their accounts with Mr Hudson, who they have been informed, has been prevented from sooner having the assistance of Mr Allport. Mr Allport has been here this week and promises to return on Saturday first, to complete his examination of the accounts, when the Directors have no doubt they will be able to have them finally closed, and that Mr Hudson will furnish them with the means of paying the Dividends, a considerable portion of which he has already paid them for this purpose.

Letter to an Editor

The following letter to the Editor of the *Newcastle Daily Journal*, from "A Holder of Ten Shares", was published on 23 March 1850. No comment is needed:

> Sir, the Traffic Returns of the N & CR are, as you state, very satisfactory but there can be no doubt that this line could be worked far more economically by the London & N. Western Rly. Co. than it is at present; and as there can now be no possible motive to consider what the effect of such an arrangement would be on the York, Newcastle & Berwick Company, I should strongly recommend the proprietors of the Carlisle Company to open a negotiation with the L & NWR—not for a lease, but for a working agreement similar to that which subsists between the latter company and the Lancaster & Carlisle Railway; its dividend might by this means be increased one per cent.

The Fifties

The 1850s were generally years of consolidation by the N & CR; the branch line to Alston opened in 1852 (see chapter 3), traffic increased, while revenue and dividends remained highly satisfactory. The company continued to provide a good service to the area it served, linking east and west coast routes but staying independent of both. But its allegiance, through history, was probably more to the east coast, and when the York,

Newcastle & Berwick Railway became the greater North Eastern Railway, it seemed a matter of time before the N & CR became a part of the North Eastern network. In fact the eventual link-up took several years of preliminaries, and was only accomplished with some difficulty, as will be related.

In the early 1850s, the N & CR was intent on improving its line and rolling stock. An important matter was the laying of better rails to meet the increasing size of locomotives in particular. In 1850–1 the 31 miles between Blenkinsopp and Ryton was relaid and by 1853 the old 42lb/yd and 52lb/yd rails had all gone. An accident on 3 August 1851 at Haltwhistle when a train was derailed on old rails was followed by the Government Inspector recommending the whole section to be replaced as soon as possible by heavier rails (at the cost of £20,000). The new rails weighed 60, 64 or 75lb/yd. In 1856 fish-plated rails became the standard for relayings instead of rails joined on a chair. By March 1853 the electric telegraph was in full operation on the N & CR allowing better operating and punctuality of traffic. The N & CR obtained an enviable reputation for the punctuality of its trains.

Between December 1852 and December 1853, four new 6-coupled locomotives, Nos 35–8, were delivered, two each from Hawthorns and Stephensons. These, and all further N & CR locomotives, had boiler pressure of 110lb/sq in, and 15in × 22in cylinders. No 35 was named *Prudhoe*, No 36 *Naworth*, No 37 *Blenkinsop* and No 38 *Bywell*. In 1853 Nos 1, 7, and 12 were sold out of service. No 4 was scrapped at around the same period. No 13 was rebuilt as a 2–4–0 in August 1853. In the same year no less than 325 new wagons and vans were added to stock, and another 150 mineral wagons were ordered. Locomotive No 5 was rebuilt in November 1852 with a new boiler and 5ft 0in wheels. A new locomotive shed was built at London Road, Carlisle in 1854.

Further old locomotives were rebuilt—No 24 in December 1854, No 18 in October 1855, and No 17 in May 1857. Four new 6-coupled locomotives were delivered in 1855. No 39 *Dilston* and No 40 *Langley* (Hawthorns Nos 910/1) cost £2250 each. No 41

Thirlwall and No 42 *Lanercost* were from Stephenson's (Nos 987/8) at £2220 apiece. Withdrawn were Nos 8 and 9 by September 1857, by which time No 4 *Hercules* and No 43 *Featherstonehaugh* had come from Hawthorns (Nos 992/3). The re-use of the number 4 was the first time that a new locomotive had taken the number and name of one withdrawn. No further new locomotives came until 1860, but in 1858 Nos 2 and 11 were sold. No 2 went back to Hawthorns, its builders, for £275; No 11 was sold to J. Anderson, a contractor, for £185.

Services on the line changed very little in the 1850s, at least as far as passenger trains were concerned. The service in 1854 consisted of a weekday service of four trains in each direction along the whole line, with two Sunday trains each way. A fifth weekday service was between Newcastle and Hexham, serving the section with the highest population. Greater use of third-class coaches was common after 1854, recognising the demand for cheap transport. In some cases the third-class accommodation was actually added at certain stations, such as the 6.00pm train from Carlisle as far as Milton on Saturdays only; to the 7.30am from Carlisle at Hexham, as far as Blaydon, and to the 7.00pm between Newcastle and Blaydon only. In 1858 the Border Counties Railway opened to Hexham (see Chapter 4) and it connected with trains for Newcastle. At this date there was a semi-official station at Mickley, which was used only by certain trains on certain days, and was not *officially* a station. Presumably miners made use of this "halt", as the important Mickley Colliery was nearby. Yet Mickley retained this "special" station, up to World War I or later. At Haltwhistle, good connecting was necessary with Alston branch services, but at Newcastle and Carlisle, there was little regard for the timetables of other companies. It was impossible to please both ends, so why bother, seems to have been the rule.

The N & CR was long involved in negotiations with the West Coast companies, the Lancaster & Carlisle Railway (from 1859 the London & North Western Railway), and Caledonian Railway, for the use of Citadel station. Unfortunately, the negotiations proved long, difficult, often acrimonious and fruitless. Possibly the Caledonian never forgave the N & CR for spurning its overtures of 1848. The N & CR did not help matters by arranging with the Glasgow & South Western Railway for through tickets between Newcastle and Glasgow via Dumfries. The G & SW had managed to obtain entry to Citadel, and omnibuses were provided to carry through passengers between London Road and Citadel stations; the through tickets included the $\frac{1}{2}$-mile omnibus journey.

The long wrangle over N & CR entry to Citadel is unworthy of much further discussion. The N & CR never did reach Citadel, which for Carlisle's first railway does seem to have been something of a slight. Basically, in the early 1850s the N & CR offered a fixed annual rent of £500 plus any expenses not exceeding £250 per annum. The Lancaster & Carlisle wanted £500 for the first year of entry, £750 for the second and £1000 each year thereafter, which seems excessive. Talks on this broke down in March 1855. Sporadic communications on the subject did not lessen the West Coast intransigence.

The Last Years

The Directors' Report at the annual general meeting of 16 March 1858 provides insight into the company's position and activities at the closing of its individual history. The N & CR board at that time, and it was unchanged in 1862, was as follows:

William Woods (*Chairman*), Newcastle
P. H. Howard (*Vice-Chairman*), Corby Castle
Matthew Anderson, Newcastle
George Clayton Atkinson, Wylam Hall
John Blenkinsopp Coulson, Swinburne Castle
Isaac Crawhall, Thorpe Green
William Dunn, Newcastle
John Fogg Elliott, Elvet Hill, Durham

Henry Liddell, Long Benton, Newcastle
John Ramshay, Naworth Castle (representing the Earl of Carlisle)

The secretary remained the long-serving John Adamson, and the manager Henry Smiles. It will be noted that the important landed gentry remained represented on the board to the end.

The report contains much useful information on the state of the N & CR in 1857. Passenger traffic receipts were £48,329 13s 0d; goods traffic receipts £49,557 18s 3d; coal and mineral traffic £68,964 16s 1d; cattle traffic £4581 4s 11d; parcels, horses, carriages traffic £3155 0s 2d; mails £1000 0s 0d; wagon rents £3282 18s 10d; rents of property £593· 10s 4d. (Total nett receipts worked out at £103,217.) The number of passenger miles run was 227,303, and goods/mineral miles 482,508. The total rolling stock was 37 locomotives (classified as 23 goods, 11 passenger and three pilot), having an average consumption of coke at 38.03lb/mile. The other stock was as follows:

Passenger carriages	
first-class	11
composite	6
second-class	24
third-class	44
Passenger train vans—	8
horse boxes	13
carriage trucks	9
goods train vans	15
goods trucks, 5-ton	169
goods trucks, 3-ton	176
corn trucks	92
cattle trucks	77
coke trucks	176
stone wagons	95
coal wagons, 6-ton	80
chaldron coal wagons	2301

130 additional chaldron coal wagons had arrived, at the cost of £3769 4s 0d, in the year. Numerous details of expenses and salaries were listed, and examples include:

	£	s	d
Expenses			
station clerks, guards, porters	9161	4	6
horse keep, harnesses, etc.	741	4	8
fuel and gas	419	12	8
oil and general stores	265	2	2
printing and stationery	575	3	8
rent of quay at Blaydon	19	0	0
platelayers wages	5602	14	10
salary, secretary and clerks	1910	18	10
repairs of roads, bridges etc.	474	18	3
repairs of stations	553	13	9
repairs of works, coke ovens etc.	1094	7	1
auditors' salaries	100	0	0
superintendents' and inspectors' wages	633	4	6

The report mentions two works affecting the N & CR. "The line of the Border Counties Railway from the junction near Hexham to Chollerford, is drawing to a completion, and steps are being taken by that Company to carry on with Energy the works on the remaining portion of the Line which will open out an important Mineral District and contribute to the traffic of this Railway to a very fair extent at no distant period. In the course of the last Summer, the new Dock at Maryport was opened for general businesses and the Dock at Silloth is reported to be progressing most favourably, no difficulties having arisen in the construction." The N & CR hoped for increased traffic as a result of the opening of the two docks at Maryport and Silloth.

In 1858, the N & CR began to have some of its locomotives burn coal instead of coke, to reduce expenses (regardless of the conditions in the Act of 1835) although the company's Derwenthaugh coke ovens had been doubled in 1852. The use of coal so reduced costs of fuel that by 1862 it was virtually complete on the line. The coke ovens were later sold to a private operator, since they were of no further use to the railway.

Union with the North Eastern

The North Eastern Railway, combining the York, Newcastle & Berwick, the Leeds & Thirsk, and the York & North Midland Railways, had become a powerful and prosperous railway within a few years. The N & CR shareholders, not forgetting their own brief unfulfilled "union" with the YNB in 1848–9, soon were contrasting the good dividends of their N & CR with the excellent ones of the NER, and amalgamation discussion was natural. By 1858 chairman William Woods had with the directors' and shareholders' backing given the NER a proposal for a union. The NER chairman, H. S. Thompson, wrote to Woods on 16 November 1858, thus:

Dear Sir,

Your offer was laid before our Board on Friday and as soon as it was explained to them that the terms involved a considerable payment to you beyond the share which would naturally accrue to you by making past receipts the basis of division for the future, they declined to consider it further, and I am requested to report to you our regret that we should have failed in explaining to you the precise nature of our proposal. The matter originated with members of your own Board, and whatever might have been their views, it was very far from *our* intention to try to induce you to part with your line against your own convictions, and to offer you a fancy price for it.

. . . we consider that in consequence of the new schemes North and South of the Tyne which either have been or probably will be proposed to Parliament, it will shortly be necessary for the old Companies to choose their friends, and to make such alliances as will as far as possible, secure them against all comers. It appears to us that if this is an important and desirable object for the North Eastern Co., it is *at least as much so* for the Newcastle & Carlisle Co. and therefore that the principal reason for a union between the companies is one which offers fully as strong an inducement for the smaller Company to unite with the larger as for the larger to join the smaller.

The most important point connected with such an arrangement is the bearing which it would have on the receipts of each Company.

The traffic of the North Eastern increases more rapidly than that of the Newcastle & Carlisle Co. consequently a union between the two Companies based upon the past would give a decided advantage to your Company. This advantage our Company is willing to concede in consideration of the increased security and form of improved working afforded by the union, but whilst we are offering to give one advantage in exchange for another, you are only asked to accept of both *increased security and improved receipts.*

On 27 November J. Cleghorn, NER secretary, wrote to Woods that (Thompson) "is glad to find that the Newcastle & Carlisle Board have reappointed a Committee to discuss the subject of amalgamation, and that our Board yesterday also re-appointed the Committee who formerly had the matter in hand, to meet and confer with the N & C Committee whenever they find it convenient to do so". Soon after, Henry Tennant, NER accountant at Newcastle, wrote to Henry Smiles that the NER's idea of the proportion for amalgamation was "on the basis of the Carlisle Company receiving 9.75% of the joint net receipts of the united company". The N & CR Committee considered 10% was a fairer figure, and Woods communicated this fact to Thompson on 28 December.

On 7 February 1859, Henry Smiles issued the following notice to the Shareholders from the N & CR board room, Newcastle Central station:

In consequence of increased competition and the probable effect of new Lines which are at present in progress, and other schemes which may shortly be brought before Parliament, the Directors have considered that it would conduce greatly to the stability of this Company, and the permanent interests of the Shareholders, if an amalgamation with the North Eastern Railway Company were effected.

In 1859, the N & CR was finding itself in the centre of railway intrigue. The North British Railway was expanding, casting its eyes into England and with particular emphasis on reaching both Carlisle and Newcastle; the Border Counties Railway was to be its link with Newcastle. The powerful London & North

Western Railway was taking-over its northern extension, the Lancaster & Carlisle, and also had a vision of reaching Newcastle and the north-east generally. With these pressures, the N & CR was being drawn towards its friendly fellow occupier of the Newcastle Central Station, the NER.

Smiles told the shareholders:

> The Directors have given their most serious consideration to this matter, and the terms agreed upon, subject to the sanction of the Shareholders, are based upon the relative net receipts of the two companies in the years 1855, 1856 and 1857, subject to certain modifications which the peculiar circumstances of each Company seemed to require, the proportion of this Company being $\frac{1}{10}$ of the joint net profits. The Directors feel that the interchange of traffic which will result from this consolidation of interests, will prove advantageous to the trade of the two Districts, as the opening of new sources of revenue and the economy of a united management will be beneficial to the Shareholders of the amalgamated Companies. It is proposed to apply for an Act for the necessary legal powers in the Session of 1860, and in the meanwhile to carry out the objects of the Amalgamation by a working agreement to be considered as taking effect from the 1st of January of the present year.

The very haste of so establishing a working agreement perhaps indicates the other pressures that the N & CR and NER were aware of. Woods, in a special report to the shareholders on amalgamation, dated 21 February 1859, said that "Your Directors believe the terms provisionally agreed upon to be fair to both Companies and mutually advantageous, whilst to the N & C Company a larger dividend with increased stability will be secured by the Amalgamation". The word "stability" is interesting, because both NBR and LNWR were trying to get support on the N & CR board and with shareholders, against the amalgamation.

The 10% proportion of the N & CR is well above that which figures for 1855–7 show, and indicates the NER's sudden desire to secure the Carlisle line.

Year	Company	Receipts	%
1855	NER	£861,828	–
	N & CR	£ 94,667	(9.89%)
1856	NER	£940,742	–
	N & CR	£100,867	(9.68%)
1857	NER	£991,263	–
	N & CR	£103,217	(9.43%)

On 8 March 1859 John Irving, a director of the Silloth Dock Company and a NBR supporter, wrote to the N & CR shareholders saying that the amalgamation would be injurious to them. He asserted that the NER had diverted traffic away from the N & CR to go by its own lines, whenever possible, eg "It is a proved fact that the Sunderland and Carlisle traffic has gone round by Leeds and Lancaster instead of the direct route by Newcastle. It has been admitted that the Liverpool and Newcastle traffic amounting to 14,000 tons a year has been purposely driven from their line by the Directors for a subsidy from the North Eastern of about £1100, and that your own Manager when applied to for rates, advises Liverpool goods to be sent by the North Eastern as the cheapest route." Irving calculated "from the published reports of both Companies and making allowance for the adjustment of Mails, the gross receipts per mile of the North Eastern have been: 1855 £2401; 1856 £2501 (increase £100); 1857 £2568 (increase £67); while those of the Newcastle & Carlisle have been, per mile in 1855 £2133; 1856 £2238 (increase £105); 1857 £2292 (increase £54). The North Eastern traffic has been carefully and skilfully cultivated, and at the expense of the Newcastle & Carlisle, while the traffic of the Newcastle & Carlisle has been studiously kept down."

Nevertheless, the working agreement went ahead, and soon a close co-operation developed, especially at Newcastle Central Station and Forth goods station. By June 1859, the NER general manager, W. O'Brien, could write to Henry Smiles from York, almost as a regional deputy: "If you could conveniently come

Stations – 2 *Above*: Brampton Junction in 1971 – view to the east. (*Author*).
Below: Station buildings at Riding Mill. (*Author*).

Stations – 3 *Above*: Looking east at Scotswood (N&CR) in 1948. (*H. Gordon Tidey, courtesy British Rail*). *Below*: Hexham station from the west. (*Author*).

over and see me on Saturday morning I should be obliged to you to do so—the three points on which I wish to talk to you are:

1. The arrangement with the Border Counties Railway for the use of Hexham Station.
2. The practicability of unloading all our Cattle at your Cattle landing place so as to avoid the necessity of driving them through the town, and the possibility of making some additional charge for this—I wish you would see Mr Allan on this subject tomorrow.
3. The result of your interview with Mr Fisher and the best steps to be taken for putting an end to our Agreements as to Belfast and Liverpool traffic with Newcastle."

Mr Allan was the NER Northern Division Goods Manager.

The Act of Union

The amalgamation act was passed on 17 July 1862 (*25–6 Vic c145*), after over two years of effort, including defeat in the 1861 Session, the LNWR and NBR in particular showing great determination to thwart it in pursuit of their own ambitions in the North East. The NER only achieved the Act by granting concessions to these companies, and their opposition and rival schemes melted away. (For details, see *The Railways of Consett and North West Durham* David & Charles 1971.) Also, the NER made an agreement with the West Coast companies, for it to use Carlisle Citadel station.

CHAPTER 3

The Alston Branch

1850–1976

This chapter was commenced soon after the closure of the Alston branch railway on 1 May 1976. The line had survived the Beeching axe, but it was hopelessly uneconomic. However, the South Tynedale Railway Preservation Society exists to try to preserve all or part of the line and run it as a service and tourist attraction. Had the line closed ten or twenty years earlier, there would have been regrets, but no such society, a phenomenon really of the late 1960s onwards. (See Chapter 10.)

Returning to the mid-19th century, the northern Pennines had a prosperous lead mining industry which suffered in many areas from poor transportation facilities. Very early on, the New-castle & Carlisle directors had considered a branch railway to the Alston area to provide easy access to the local lead mines and smelters in the Hexham/Haydon Bridge region, such as Langley, which were sending ore and refined lead by packhorse, or in carts where a good road existed. There was a particularly large movement of ore to Whitfield (West Allendale) and Dukesfield, and to the Blaydon refinery on Tyneside.

The Nenthead Project

From the first opening of the N & CR in 1835 lead was an import-ant traffic commodity. In 1841 the London Lead Company, which dominated the industry around Alston, stated that it was saving between £700–£800 annually by the use of available rail-

72

ways near its operations. Any further saving was always welcome to the British lead producers, as foreign imports of lead were highly competitive. Much construction of turnpike roads in the Hexham–Alston region had been encouraged by the lead producers from the late 18th century. The London Lead Company's chief smelter was at Langley, south of Haydon Bridge, and the LLC sent ore by road to Haltwhistle station, thence by rail to Haydon Bridge or Hexham for transit to Tyneside. It was the long road haulage down the South Tyne Valley from Alston to Haltwhistle, which soon persuaded the LLC to discuss a branch railway with the N & CR. Certainly, times were prosperous. In 1840 the Northern Pennines as a whole produced 7000 tons of lead per year from about 60 mines. Alston parish, much of it high moorland and fells, had over 6000 people, and the bleaker Nenthead district had some 2000.

The N & CR sent John Blackmore and assistants to survey the area for a line, but the financial depression of 1841–2 prevented progress otherwise. By 1845 conditions had ameliorated and the idea of a South Tyne branch railway was approved by the N & CR Board. A line could be made from a junction at Haltwhistle station, following closely the South Tyne river up to Alston, and then along Nentdale to Nenthead. A long steady gradient would be needed, as the line would rise from about 380ft above sea level, to 1400ft at Nenthead, in almost 18 miles' distance. An item of some expense would be the need for numerous bridges, some of considerable size, over the South Tyne and its many tributary streams.

A Bill was drawn up and presented to Parliament at the same time as another Bill for a branch in the North Tyne valley (also primarily aimed at mineral transport). The Bill was passed on 26 August 1846 (9–10 Vic c394) but the North Tyne Bill suffered defeat. A capital of £240,000 was authorised for the Nenthead branch, to be raised by the sale of shares, with a further £80,000 by loans. Work did not get under way at once because the precise course of the line at certain places was contested by landowners who wanted minimum inconvenience. In particular, Messrs

Cuthbert Ellison and the Hon James Hope Wallace were demanding. The difficulties may be judged to a certain extent from the following N & CR notice in the *Newcastle Journal* of 13 November 1847 which is headed:

Newcastle & Carlisle Railway. Alteration of Branch. Notice is hereby given that Application is intended to be made to Parliament in the ensuing Session, for an Act to alter, amend and enlarge, the Powers and Provisions of an Act passed in the Session held in the 9th and 10th Years of the Reign of the present Majesty Queen Victoria entituled [*sic*] "An Act to authorize the Newcastle-upon-Tyne & Carlisle Railway Company to extend their Railway, in Newcastle-upon-Tyne, to make a Branch Railway, and for other Purposes connected with their undertaking".

Then come details, and the basic Nenthead Branch changes can be outlined as follows. The old line was to be abandoned between Haltwhistle station and Broomhouse Meadows (Bellister) on the land of Cuthbert Ellison, and to be re-aligned to avoid the Ellison domain. Also

abandoning so much of the branch railway by the said Act authorised to be made, as extends between a Close belonging to the Honorable James Hope Wallace, in the Occupation of George Proud, in the Township of Featherstone . . . and a Close belonging to the said James Hope Wallace in the Occupation of William Ridley, in the Township of Knaresdale.

The notice concludes thus:

Also, powers to purchase by Compulsion or otherwise, Lands and Houses for the purposes aforsaid, and to vary or extinguish all Rights and Privileges in any manner connected with such Lands and Houses, or which would in any manner impede or interfere with the construction or maintenance of the said Railway and Works. And also to extend the Time limited by the said Act for carrying the same into effect.

10 November 1847 Claytons & Dunn
Adamson & Sons
Solicitors to the N & CR Co.

However, the railway mania and its aftermath had temporarily sapped public confidence in railway management, and the general economic lethargy meant that the South Tyne line saw little progress in 1848; the new Act was not obtained, so staking-out the route was impossible. The frustration of the London Lead Company can be imagined. Delay was also caused by the leasing of the N & CR by the York, Newcastle & Berwick Railway in 1848, but there was no intention of dropping the scheme. Two newspaper advertisements in 1849 indicate hopefulness. On 17 March: "The contractors of the Alston Branch of the Newcastle & Carlisle Railway have made a donation of £2 2s 0d (£2.10) to the Newcastle Infirmary" (anticipating future needs?); while on 13 October: "Crown Inn, Alston, To Let, (at May Day 1850) The Alston Branch of the Newcastle & Carlisle Railway now in the course of making will shortly be completed, and will materially increase the Trade and Population of the Town and Neighbourhood of Alston". In fact by this date only preliminary work had begun, but no doubt the need for a new licensee allowed slight distortions.

The amended Bill was presented to Parliament in 1849, receiving the Royal Assent on 13 July (*12–12 Vic c43*). The route as amended had been altered in six places and in addition, a short "branch of the branch" was the Lambley Fell branch, about one mile in length, to connect with the Earl of Carlisle's Brampton Railway at Lambley, allowing Tindale Fells coal and lime to reach the Alston line. Lead ore could be sent also to the Hartleyburn smelter on the Tindale Fells.

The line was now referred to as the "Alston Branch", because the short rather steep 4-mile section from Alston to Nenthead was dropped. Since the whole region south of Alston had lead activities, it was thought unnecessary to especially single out Nenthead. Alston would be the terminal. It was the chief settlement, the focus of the region, the market town. The cost of the last four miles was not considered necessary.

Built at Last

Staking-out was soon done, in late 1849, but contracts for the construction were let in 1850. The line was planned to be single track, with space for a second line of rails to be allowed in certain sections, notably the Haltwhistle end. As Tomlinson stated:

> The works . . . were necessarily heavy, comprising a cutting about a mile long through the manor of Bellister, and a number of stone viaducts, three over the South Tyne, and the others over the Glendue, Thinhope, Knar, Thornhope, Whitley and Gilderdale Burns. Of these, the highest was the Lambley viaduct, which crossed the vale of the South Tyne on nine semi-circular arches of 58 foot span, at a height of 110 feet above the surface of the water. There were gradients on the branch as steep as 1 in 56, 1 in 70 and 1 in 80.

The stone for the bridges was an attractive sandstone, much being brought from a quarry beside the N & CR at Fourstones. Contract No 3 of the branch stated: "All the stone to be used for the work of this Contract shall be stone from Prudham . . . or other stone approved of by the Engineer."

As early as March 1851, the $4\frac{1}{4}$ miles from Haltwhistle to Shaft Hill were opened for goods traffic. The junction at Haltwhistle faced westwards, at the east end of the station, the branch reaching Haltwhistle by a very long curve, much in the Bellister cutting and rather steep at 1 in 80, then crossing the South Tyne by a fine six-arch stone viaduct, built for two lines of rails, and its foundations made with the knowledge of the need for firmness. Hereabouts, periodic floods of the river, and the friction caused by the carrying of all kinds of pebbles and boulders, required a very firm bridge.

Work proceeded all the way to Alston and some stone from quarries in that neighbourhood was used for the contract for that stretch of line. The graceful, lofty viaduct at Lambley, built to carry only a single line, was the major work, and was the last to be finished. On 19 July 1851, a passenger service commenced between Haltwhistle and Shaft Hill with an intermediate station

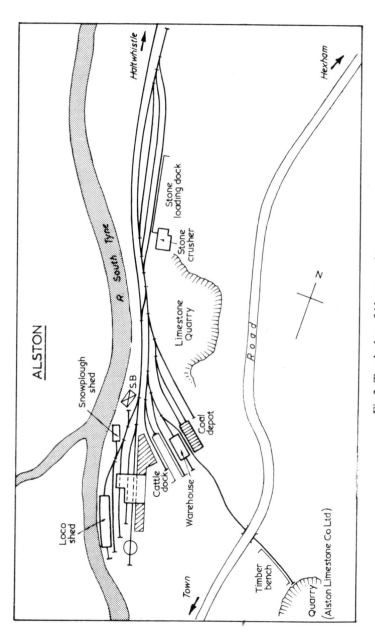

Fig 3 Track plan of Alston station

at Featherstone, actually close to the hamlet of Rowfoot. Always to be a feature of the line, the branch passenger service connected with the main line service at Haltwhistle.

On 1 January 1852, the Lambley Fell branch and the $8\frac{1}{2}$ miles of line from Alston to Lambley station were opened for goods traffic. Only when Lambley viaduct was completed could a link be made across the South Tyne to Shaft Hill, and on 17 November 1852 the viaduct was declared open and services on the whole branch began. The London Lead Company and other local industries (such as lime makers), and the population of the Alston area, had easy access to the N & CR main line and all its connections.

At least one person gave his life in the building of Lambley viaduct, undoubtedly one of the North-East's most attractive railway bridges, with its graceful nine arches and 110ft 0in maximum height. A verdict of accidental death was returned on Peter Feck, aged 27, by a Hexham Coroner's Court, on 10 July 1851.

> It appeared that the deceased had been engaged at the Lambley Viaduct on the Alston branch of the Newcastle and Carlisle Railway, in lowering a stone to the bottom of the viaduct by means of crane, when the chain broke, in consequence of which the deceased fell from the crane at a height of 60 feet, and died shortly afterwards.

Early Services and Activities

The line had been built primarily to carry minerals, particularly lead and coal. However, from the 1850s the lead mining industry was commencing a steady decline, although the Tindale Fells coal mining industry was to enjoy a much longer prosperity. Passenger train services were adequate for what was, after all, not a very densely populated district. At first there were only two trains each way except on Sundays. For example, in 1858 departures from Haltwhistle were at 8.38am and 7.00pm, arriving at Alston at 9.26am and 7.48pm respectively. Departures from Alston at 7.28am and 5.28pm, arriving at Haltwhistle, were at

8.16am and 6.16pm. Thus there was no difference in time whether uphill or downhill, and an average speed of 17mph! Fares between termini were 2s 9d (14p) first-class, 2s 0d (10p) second-class, 1s 5d (7p) third-class. The intermediate stations were at Featherstone (much later renamed Featherstone Park), Lambley, and Slaggyford. The original temporary station at Shaft Hill was not used after the whole line was open, and thus local inhabitants had to cross the river to reach Lambley, although some years later in the 1890s a station was again provided at this spot, possibly because of local requests for one.

Connections at Haltwhistle were as good as possible considering there were only five main line trains each way at this time. For example, the 8.16am arrival at Haltwhistle allowed a departure for Carlisle at 8.20am and for Newcastle at 8.36am. Since Alston was in the county of Cumberland it had need of as good communication with Carlisle, the county town, as with Tyneside. There was no passenger service on the Lambley Fell branch. By 1870 a third train each way had been added to the Alston service.

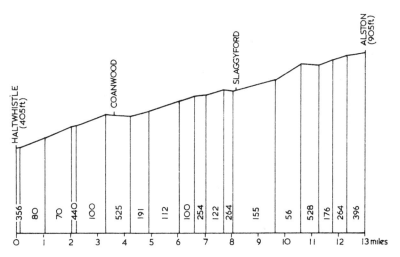

Fig 4 Gradient profile of Alston branch

Station houses and other buildings provided at the branch stations were largely of the usual sandstone, but waiting rooms were often of wood. Passing loops for trains were put in at the intermediate stations, where only one platform was provided. At Alston station somewhat superior facilities were emphasised by an all-over roof to the one regular platform. A locomotive shed here was provided for the one or two locomotives allotted specifically to branch duties.

NER Improvements

After 1862, when the NER inherited the line with the takeover of the N & CR, the new owner in its efficient way was soon assessing the needs of the line and improvements to assist traffic on it. In May 1868 the Way and Works Committee ordered that additional accommodation "for the loading of cattle and sheep be provided at Alston Station as recommended by the Traffic Committee at a cost not exceeding £20". The line had been built with a view to lucrative mineral traffic but the NER was not going to neglect the basic agricultural resource of the district. In May 1872 the station "shed roof" was ordered to be reconstructed, a tender of £446 13s 4d (£446.67) being accepted, but in May 1873 it was noted that £62 3s 2d (£62.16) was the extra cost for "Alston station improvements".

Earlier, in February 1866 it was agreed to spend £33 capital for "a small office to be erected in the Goods Warehouse at Alston". At the junction at Haltwhistle traffic was such that in February 1865 the NER ordered a 42ft turntable at a cost of £360 "in place of the present one which is insufficient for the requirements of that station". Much later, in 1881–2, some £120 was spent on new station buildings at Lambley.

The provision of a station at Shaft Hill (later Coanwood), mentioned earlier, came in 1877–8. At the end of 1877 it was reported that £672 had been expended on the works for "Shafthill New Station". As with the other intermediate stations, the use of wood for the station buildings was a characteristic.

Mixed Fortunes

The once-booming lead mining activities in the Northern Pennines began to decline sharply from the 1870s which was unfortunate for the Alston line, but coal mining in the Lambley region was reasonably prosperous, although here again, around the turn of the century there were signs of decline. Stone, lime and agricultural traffic were small but steady. The Alston Lime Company had in 1876 opened depots for the sale of its lime, at Heaton (Newcastle) and Gateshead. Passenger traffic grew slowly, and in the bad winters in particular, the railway was the "lifeline" for Alston as a link with civilisation, a factor mentioned in the 1960s when the subject of closure was being mooted.

In 1880 there were three daily passenger trains along the branch each way (not Sundays), and a Saturday extra each way. The single fare from Haltwhistle to Alston was 2s 4d (11½p) first-class, 1s 9d (9p) second-class, and 1s 1d (5½p) third-class. A third-class ticket from Alston to Newcastle in 1887 cost 4s 2d (21p), and to Carlisle 3s 0d (15p). Generally, reasonable connections were always provided with both east- and west-bound trains at Haltwhistle although there was sometimes a fair wait. A regular Sunday service of two trains each way was established early in the next century, which seems commendable in view of the decline in population of the Alston area (only 3000 people in the parish by 1911). By this period, Featherstone station had been given the addition of "Park", and Shafthill was re-named Coanwood in April 1885. The NER did its best to boost the line's traffic, in view of the scenic nature of South Tyneside. In 1906 "Holiday Contract Tickets" were issued at all NER stations from Hexham to Carlisle, giving two weeks' travel on the NER west of Hexham for £1.50 (first-class) and £1.00 (third-class).

In 1886 only 2000 tons of lead were produced in the Alston district, and decline continued thereafter, but at the same period of time 20,000 tons of coal per year were being received at Lambley on the Lambley Fell Branch, from Thompson & Sons

Tindale Fells collieries. Also, limeworks and coke ovens in that area boosted mineral traffic. In 1895 the total traffic at Lambley for coal, coke, lime and limestone, was 48,566 tons. Unfortunately there was a severe decline just over a year later, as some mines became exhausted. The Lambley coal traffic received from the local mines was 16,805 tons in 1906, 13,333 tons in 1907 and 3630 tons in 1908, falling to 18 tons in 1909. In fact, Lambley colliery had closed in 1908, and the "Kirkhouse Branch" section of the line (ie that part of the Earl of Carlisle's Railway) from Lambley (NER Lambley Fell Branch) to Midgeholme, was closed, so all Tindale coal thence had to be sent to Brampton.

Other metalliferous ores were produced in the Alston district, and provided a variable traffic. Zinc ores were perhaps the chief item. These ores gave 8604 tons of traffic at Alston station in 1906, and 9873 tons in 1914.

General goods traffic was heaviest at Alston. In 1910 Alston's goods receipts (exclusive of livestock) were £3238, but the other stations managed only £100 at Coanwood, £64 Slaggyford, £40 Lambley, and £38 Featherstone Park. The loss of mineral traffic is reflected in the comparison of total receipts for Lambley station in 1900 (£3565) and 1910 (£392).

Wagonloads of livestock despatched from the five stations in 1908 were: Alston 328, Slaggyford 104, Lambley 22, Coanwood 6, Featherstone Park 48. Alston station in fact received more from parcels than animals—£594 against £269 in 1910, for example.

Thus, by World War I the Alston branch had declined almost to the general level of importance of the Allendale Railway not far away, a rather unprofitable rural branch line. Only a certain amount of mineral and agricultural traffic redeemed it, which the motor age was to take later. Also, the great number of stone bridges requiring maintenance did not make it a railway low on expenses.

CHAPTER 4

The Border Counties Railway

The Northern Raider

The early plans for a railway extending from the new N & CR northwards into Scotland were not forgotten during the late 1840s, when such plans seemed to have lapsed. Many people on Tyneside, in the Northumberland fastness of the North Tyne (Tynedale as it once was named), and in the Scottish Borders wanted a railway link. Surveyors had tramped the sparsely-peopled valleys and uplands and all the proposals had come to nought—or so it seemed. But an inland Anglo-Scottish line was in fact to come, and when it did come it was to be a most unusual, distinctive and picturesque line. It was the Border Counties Railway.

The Border Counties Railway scheme was promoted in 1853, at Hexham, for a railway from the N & CR at or near Hexham, up the North Tyne valley to the Bellingham area and beyond. The very title of the railway, "Border Counties", reveals its intention of going beyond Northumberland. It is difficult to say whether the North British Railway company was behind the BCR from its outset, but it is possible. However, in the early years the NBR kept outside the picture, revealing its interest only when it had to. Ostensibly the BCR was an attempt by a group of Hexham area gentry to extend the benefits of a railway to the people and population of Tynedale. The leader of the promoters was W. H. Charlton of Hesleyside, near Bellingham. The BCR Bill received the Royal Assent on 31 July 1854 (*17–18 Vic c212*) authorising a capital of £250,000 by shares and £83,333 by loans, for a line 26 miles in length from Hexham to Plashetts.

83

Plashetts was chosen as terminus because of the known coal deposits there, whose extent and value was emphasised in the BCR prospectus. How early Charlton envisaged a northward extension from Plashetts into Scotland is unknown, but as John Thomas has pointed out in *The North British Railway* (Vol 1), "Charlton was no stranger at Carham Hall and it was natural that the railway-promoting Border squires got their heads together". (Carham was the seat of Richard Hodgson, NBR chairman.) Hodgson was planning an extension of his Edinburgh–Hawick branch to Carlisle, and a possible link with the BCR if the latter went north of Plashetts.

After the Act, the BCR scheme took some time to get under way, due partly to difficulties with certain landowners on the route. At last on 11 December 1855 the chairman, Mr Charlton, cut the first sod at Hexham, and work progressed, slowly during winter, and then more rapidly in 1856. William Hutchinson, the contractor, obtained stone for the works at local quarries near Barrasford and Chollerton. The line was intended to be usually single track, and a branch from near Bellingham to Ridsdale ironworks was at first intended, but then dropped. The line left the N & CR at Border Counties Junction, one mile west of Hexham, immediately crossing the Tyne to reach the north bank, and to follow the east bank of the North Tyne northwards. Hexham viaduct gave trouble. The contract to build this bridge and three others, the Rede, Erring Burn and Prestwick Burn bridges, was granted to Hutchinson in August 1855. This contract specified their completion by 31 July 1857 on pain of £30 per week thereafter forfeited by the contractor if not finished. Hexham viaduct was

> to consist of three large and three smaller openings across the which the Railway is to be carried by wrought iron girders supported on cast iron standards. The Main Girders of the large openings being 80 feet clear from support to support, and those of the smaller openings 60 feet clear.

This single-line bridge crossed the river obliquely and required very deep foundations to withstand the periodic spating of the river. Hutchinson had some trouble in building it, as the river itself tended to interfere with the foundation work. North of the viaduct, the line followed the North Tyne closely, winding continually, but affording when it opened out marvellous views of the river and valley. The Prestwick, Erring and Rede bridges, and many smaller bridges, were all built of stone, chiefly sandstone. The Rede viaduct, across the mouth of the river Rede at Redesmouth where that river joined the North Tyne, was built as double track. It was of sandstone "to consist of 13 small openings of 20 feet and three large openings of 57 feet clear from upright to upright" in the 1855 contract, but in fact it was actually built with a total of five arches, on an oblique line to the Rede itself.

On 5 April 1858 Hutchinson at last had the first part of the line ready, the four miles from Hexham junction to Chollerford, and it was duly opened, with an intermediate station at Wall. The section was mainly at 1 in 100 gradient. The BCR had obtained several locomotives of 2–2–2 type from Beyer, Peacock & Co to operate the trains, and it also procured its own carriages and wagons. At Hexham station the N & CR staff performed the necessary functions for BCR trains, and the BCR paid a rental for use of the station and staff. BCR passenger trains connected with N & CR Newcastle–Hexham trains. At opening, on weekdays, the BCR had four trains each way between Hexham and Chollerford, and two trains each way on Sundays. A 17-seat horse omnibus left Bellingham at 7.00am for Chollerford, and returned from Chollerford at 3.00pm. The newspaper advertisement signed by Cuthbert U. Laws, BCR Secretary, for the opening gave the Hexham–Chollerford single fare at 1s 0d (first-class), 9d (second-class) and 6d (third-class). In July 1858 the BCR and N & CR reached an agreement on through fares and rates between their lines, depending upon distance travelled on each.

Meanwhile, Hutchinson struggled on with his contract well behind the original schedule, which the BCR revised as (see the

August 1855 contract) work would have to stop altogether. On 1 December 1859 the eight miles from Chollerford to Countess Park were opened, and services extended to that place. Intermediate stations were at Chollerton, Barrasford and Wark. The latter station was over a mile from the village of Wark, which lay on the opposite bank of the North Tyne. However, it also served the village of Birtley, a mile away. All stations had a single platform, and Wark was the first to receive a passing loop.

The new section of the line was mainly at 1 in 100, 120, 130 and 150. The earthworks were not considerable but there were two large cuttings, one of a mile length, between Chollerton and Barrasford, with another at Chipchase. At Chipchase was Chipchase Castle whose owner had required the BCR to screen the line with tree plantations and with boundary walls resembling the castle architecture, somewhat increasing the expenses. At the close of 1859 £185,611 9s 10d (£185,611.49) had been spent on the BCR, including £131,026 17s 2d (£131,026.86) on construction work, and £27,057 9s 4d (£27,057.47) on land and compensation. The BCR stations were substantially built of stone, both station house and buildings. Countess Park, however, was a temporary station, to be replaced when the line was extended to Redesmouth.

The Pirate Shows its Colours

During 1859 the North British Railway at last showed its true colours. The NBR was in the process of extending southwards from Hawick, and intended to take over the BCR as part of a route to Tyneside. The NBR was hostile to the current overtures being made by the N & CR to the North Eastern Railway; the NBR would have liked to secure the N & CR for itself, or at least maintain the latter's independence. This was the great period of North British expansion; the Scottish Raider intended to take as much of Northumberland as it could. The impoverished BCR welcomed the NBR with open arms. Thus the second BCR Act of 1 August 1859, the Liddesdale Section and Deviations Act

Stations – 4 *Above*: Wylam from the east, 1971. (*Author*). *Below*: Prudhoe,
20 January 1971. (*Author*).

B1S on the N&CR *Above*: No 61395 on a down train passing Wetheral. (*J. W. Armstrong*). *Below*: No 61239 arrives at Haltwhistle bound for Newcastle on 5 September 1955. (*H. C. Casserley*).

(*22–23 Vic c43*), authorised extension of the BCR from Plashetts to Riccarton, 14 miles to the north in Roxburghshire. Riccarton was a desolate wasteland in the Southern Uplands, but the BCR was to join the North British Hawick–Carlisle extension (Border Union Railway) here, as surveys made it, by reason of relief, the only practicable junction point—lying 15 miles south of Hawick. The Border Union Railway Act had been passed on 21 July 1859 just eleven days before the BCR extension Act.

But this was not all—the NBR had a third scheme going. The country between Bellingham and Morpeth in central Northumberland was a sparsely-populated agricultural-cum-moorland expanse, an obvious area where railways should never be promoted. But the few people in the region wanted a line, and the NBR stepped in to help them. The Wansbeck Railway from the BCR at Redesmouth, eastwards to Morpeth, was supported by the NBR, and received its Act on 8 August 1859, a week after the BCR extension Act. This was Richard Hodgson's outflanking line on the NER, to join the independent Blyth & Tyne Railway at Morpeth, and allow the NBR to reach Newcastle that way. The BCR would let it reach the N & CR, and should the NER succeed in getting the N & CR, the NBR still could get to its goal, Newcastle, via the Wansbeck line. It was in view of the advent of the Wansbeck line, that the NBR saw Redesmouth as an important junction, and so authorised building of the Rede viaduct as a double track bridge. This bridge was not in fact finished until 1861. With the resources of the NBR openly backing it, the BCR line north from Countess Park was pursued more rapidly. BCR receipts from traffic from opening until 31 January 1860 were: £1578 0s 6d (£1578.03) passengers; £1817 18s 2d (£1817.91) goods.

Completion of the BCR

In February 1860 work on the line was being actively pursued between Countess Park and Thorneyburn and two thirds of this section was ready. It was hoped that all could be ready by May.

The Liddesdale section had been staked-out ready for work. The half-yearly meeting of the BCR directors at Hexham on 28 February 1860 stated the existing traffic and the hopes. An average of 3,000 passengers per month was using the Hexham–Chollerford section, "an astonishing and unexpectedly large number". The directors were particularly hopeful of heavy traffic for the Plashetts coalfield to the "southern manufacturing districts of Scotland, which were at present supplied with an inferior description of coal at fully double the price which would result as a consequence of the extension of the Border Counties Railway to Hawick". The Plashetts deposits had hitherto been little touched because of the absence of railway transport. In early 1860 £30,000 was received from the sale of 1500 shares in the Liddesdale section, and £11,000 had already been spent on preliminaries for this line.

On 13 August 1860, the NBR took over the BCR by amalgamation (Act: *23–24 Vic c195*). At this same time the NBR took over the Border Union Railway similarly, and later the Wansbeck Railway followed on 21 July 1863.

Following completion of the Rede viaduct, the NBR opened the BCR as far as Thorneyburn, on 1 February 1861, 21 miles from Hexham. Intermediate stations were opened at Reedsmouth (an example of NBR incorrect spellings), Bellingham and Tarset, and Countess Park station was closed. Another intermediate station near Hesleyside was named Charlton, after the BCR chairman. There was no real need for it, and it was closed on 1 October 1862. In September 1861, Falstone became the terminus. Work was now undertaken all the way to Riccarton, at a rapid rate. Falstone to Kielder (Keilder according to the NBR) opened on 12 May 1862, with an intermediate station at Plashetts. Near Kielder the line crossed the North Tyne for the first time after many miles of following it, by a very attractive viaduct. This sandstone viaduct was 392ft 0in long, with seven arches reaching 55ft 0in above the river. It was on lands owned by Kielder Castle (Duke of Northumberland) and within view of the castle, consequently the NBR followed the duke's ruling that it should be suitably embellished. It had battlemented parapets of baronial design and was undoubtedly the finest example of engineering on the BCR. At Kielder, the Border hills had closed in, and the frowning summits towered over the narrow gap followed by the line into Scotland.

On 21 June 1862, Captain Tyler, *RE*, a Board of Trade inspector, together with J. F. Tone, BCR and Border Union Engineer and others, inspected the Riccarton–Hawick, and Kielder–Riccarton sections, and passed them as fit for use. Gradients on the line from Reedsmouth to Kielder remained at a ruling 1 in 100, but were less severe south of Plashetts overall than the Hexham–Reedsmouth section. Between Plashetts and Kielder there were over three miles at 1 in 100. A gradient profile of the whole BCR is given in John Thomas' *The North British Railway* (Vol 1, p98).

Thus on 1 July 1862 the line was officially opened throughout, at the very same time as the Hawick–Carlisle line was opened. This last part of the BCR line had several examples of heavy engineering, in the Scottish section. There were prominent cuttings at Hudshouse Rig near a viaduct over the Dawston Burn (stone: five arches), and at Shiel Knowe near Riccarton. Near Shiel Knowe was a long embankment over a tributary stream of the Riccarton Burn. Stations opened were at Saughtree and Riccarton. Saughtree station was a mile from the tiny village of that name by the Liddel Water, and was overlooked by the massive Saughtree Fell, well over 1000ft. The BCR crossed the watershed between Tyne and Liddel Water valleys at Deadwater, at which spot a station was later in use. Riccarton station, in a barren spot amidst the high fells, had no road access and a railway village grew up here to house the NBR staff. Just south-west of Riccarton was the brooding 1464ft Arnton Fell. Between Kielder and Riccarton the BCR remained at about 1 in 100 for several miles, but with a $1\frac{1}{4}$-mile length at only 1 in 300 south of Deadwater.

NBR on Tyneside

As described earlier, the North British agreed not to oppose the amalgamation of the N & CR with the NER provided it was granted running powers from Hexham into Newcastle. This was agreed, and "Schedule B" of the N & CR–NER Amalgamation Act of 17 July 1862 stated the agreement in full:

> For all Purposes of Traffic of all kinds to and from and between all or any of the following places: To from and between Newcastle, Gateshead, Redheugh, stations of the Newcastle and Carlisle Railway Eastward of the Junction at Hexham of the Border Counties Railway . . . the Company (NER) shall at all times hereafter permit the N.B. Company with their Engines, Carriages, Waggons and Trucks, to run over, and use the Newcastle and Carlisle Railway, sidings, junctions, stations, wharves . . . and other conveniences upon that Railway between the Hexham Junction and the Central Station at Newcastle, and the station at Redheugh. The Company shall provide for the N.B. Company at the Company's Central Station at Newcastle-on-Tyne, and at the Hexham Station, proper and sufficient station accommodation, including the services of their Booking Clerks, Porters, and other Servants for the Passenger Traffic of the N.B. Company. The N.B. Company shall pay to the Company a reasonable Rent for the uses of the Station Accommodation so provided. . . ."

As is well known, the NBR granted the NER running powers between Berwick and Edinburgh as part of this same agreement. Thus both companies operated trains between Newcastle and Edinburgh by different routes. The NBR regarded its new route as a main line and advertised it as such. Its gradients between Hexham and Edinburgh, and especially on the BCR, were far heavier than the east coast route gradients. The latter was also double track throughout.

In 1869 the BCR passenger service comprised three trains each way on weekdays only, all between Newcastle and Riccarton. Thorneyburn station was only open for one train each way on Tuesdays only. One train each way omitted to stop at Saughtree and one train only called at Plashetts "when required". The journey time for Hexham–Riccarton trains was some 1 hour 50 minutes. Riccarton–Hexham took about two hours for two trains, 1 hour 47 minutes for a third.

From 1 March 1863 the NBR was allowed to run two goods trains daily each way between Forth goods station, Newcastle, and Hexham. There were goods facilities at all BCR stations except Thorneyburn. Reedsmouth station became important for goods, especially when the Wansbeck line was opened to that junction on 1 May 1865. A locomotive shed was built at Reedsmouth; another shed was at Riccarton, while NBR locomotives could use the NER shed at Hexham.

Endpieces

"MR MOSES PYE'S present Auction Appointments" heads a column in the *Newcastle Daily Journal* of 2 July 1862. And Mr Pye apparently was clearing up (for a profit) after the railway activity in the Border hills. He offered on 7 July, at "Saughtree Station, Northumberland" (a location which suggests the border has since moved southwards!) "Railway Plant, consisting of two locomotive engines, engine and saw mill, Contractors Rails, waggons, Carts & Co. at one o'clock". The following day at Kielder station more "railway plant", in this case one locomotive, contractor's rails, wagons, "dobbing carts, quarry tools & Co. at one o'clock". As a further clearance, at Falstone station, "at latter end July, more locomotives, horses, waggons, rails, cranes, winches, carts & C & C". Mr Pye concluded: "Catalogues of the Railway Plants etc., from the Auctioneer at his offices, 28 Groat Market, Newcastle, and 26 Spring Terrace, North Shields".

The advent of the Border Counties railway link is reflected for its aid to communication in the advertisement for the sale of the Bimmerhill Estate, Bellingham, on 8 July 1865. "A small Estate in North Tyne, so easily convertible into one of the most charming Summer Retreats to be found in the Border Districts of Northumberland, enjoying all of the social privileges of immediate railway Communication. In the Parish of Bellingham, containing about 78 acres of land and suitable Steading, with Southern aspect, and susceptible at comparatively little cost (the station of Charlton on the Border Counties Railway is within a few minutes walk), into a most desirable field for the experiments and valuable discoveries of the Amateur Farmer. To be put up to AUCTION by MR DONKIN at the Furnace Inn, Bellingham on Friday the 4th August, at one o'clock."

More directly, the BCR route was, in the railway age, a useful link from Tyneside to the Borders. On 13 July 1865 for example appeared a typical advertisement by the NBR in the *Newcastle Daily Journal* aimed at Tynesiders:

The joint NBR–Edinburgh & Glasgow Railway companies' advertisement offered: TOURS, 1865. "Tourist Tickets are now issued from Newcastle, Hexham, Tynemouth, Blyth and Morpeth via the Waverley Route as under:

> To Melrose and back:
> From Hexham (NBR)
>   1st class 14s 0d (70p) 2nd class 11s 0d (55p)
> From Morpeth (NBR)
>   1st class 15s 6d (77½p) 2nd class 12s 0d (60p)
> From Tynemouth (B & TR)
>   1st class 19s 0d (95p) 2nd class 14s 6d (72½p)

Traversing the wild and beautiful North Tyne valley and the Border Fells, the NBR was right to press home the scenic attractions of travel over the Border Counties and Waverley routes, the attractions which caused so many who knew to mourn both lines' closures about a century later, 13 years between each closure, leaving a vast tract of country rail-less.

Fifty Years of the BCR

Local agriculture and the sporadic local mineral traffic were important on the BCR, the former being chiefly of cattle, milk and sheep, the latter coal, iron ore (from near Bellingham, but soon exhausted), and stone. Coal traffic from Tyneside into Scotland was also significant. Passenger traffic, local population being sparse, was light. Travellers from Newcastle to Border towns, such as Galashiels, found the route convenient and attractive if they were not in a great hurry. But for Newcastle–Edinburgh traffic, those who wanted speed did not leave Newcastle by a NB train! The NB publicised the scenic charms of the area covered to north-easterners, and by offering excursion trains and special tickets won all the revenue it could. For the farming community of Tynedale and Redesdale in an age without motor vehicles, the railway was a great boon, and it had much cause to thank Mr Charlton of Hesleyside, and the NBR.

In 1869, there were three BCR passenger trains each way (all Newcastle–Riccarton) and most stations had the benefit of all, except Saughtree (only one down and two up –"down" from Newcastle), Plashetts (one down conditional), and Thorneyburn (one each way only on Tuesdays). The Reedsmouth–Morpeth service was also of three trains each way, and at Morpeth, the Blyth & Tyne gave access to Newcastle (New Bridge Street station). However, in 1874 the NER absorbed the B & T, but the NB no longer had need for worry; the N & CR access to Newcastle was excellent. On 1 March 1880 Deadwater station, right on the border, was opened officially, although an "unofficial halt" serving the few houses hereabouts, had long existed.

A slight expansion of services took place, but the basic three trains were maintained up to 1914. From 1910, however, one train each way had its terminal at Hexham (but with a NER link to Newcastle). By 1891 the NB had adjusted timetables so that some trains each way obviated the passenger changing at Riccarton. Usual termini were Hawick or Galashiels, but in the years up to almost 1910 Edinburgh itself was a common terminal. Of the six trains in 1891, three had Galashiels, one had Hawick, one Edinburgh, and one Riccarton as its northern point. Additional trains were usually run on Saturdays and Tuesdays (market days), at Newcastle (Saturday) and Hexham (both), and all between Bellingham and Hexham, to serve the small town of Bellingham, the biggest place served by the BCR. In 1910,

Riccarton was renamed "Riccarton Junction", and all BCR trains were timed to commence or terminate at the bay platform at the south end of the station. After World War I some through running northwards re-commenced. In 1913, the BCR service was as follows: down trains left Newcastle Central station at 6.07am, 10.50am, and from Hexham at 4.59pm, reaching Riccarton Junction at 8.46am, 1.36pm, and 6.34pm respectively. A daily extra ran from Reedsmouth at 3.45pm to Bellingham (returning to Reedsmouth at 4.15pm). On Saturdays extras were at 2.00pm Reedsmouth–Bellingham only, and 7.25pm Hexham–Bellingham. The up service left Riccarton Junction at 6.40am, 10.00am, and 7.10pm. The Saturday extra from Hexham returned thence from Bellingham at 2.15pm. Apart from Thorneyburn, the only BCR stations without a call were missed by the 4.59pm down from Hexham, which did not stop at Deadwater and Saughtree.

Fitting in train crossings was very necessary with limited passing points. Thus, the two early morning trains crossed at Reedsmouth, whilst the second trains met at Hexham. Obviously locomotive or other failures could cause trouble with traffic on the line, to say the least.

Noteworthy was the absence of Sunday trains. The NB directors generally were good "men o' the kirk", so Sunday was definitely a day of rest for staff and customers!

Some Goods Statistics

Goods traffic, excluding minerals, for the period 1 August 1874–31 July 1875 was as below:

Station	tons
Riccarton	5893
Saughtree	0
Kielder	327
Plashetts	735
Falstone	470
Tarset	581

Station	tons
Bellingham	1572
Reedsmouth	2363
Wark	1830
Barrasford	616
Chollerton	1095
Chollerford	1885
Wall	1326
Hexham (NB)	5387
Forth (NB)	36,727

Principal coal traffic at two dates:

	Year 1873–4 tons	Year 1909–10 tons
Riccarton	30,129	6,940
Plashetts	44,611	23,185
Wall	65,868	10,199
Hexham	7,811	30,625

The local collieries at Plashetts and Wall (Acomb) show their significance.

Goods traffic of the NB at Newcastle realised £22,367.65 in receipts in 1910, and livestock traffic was an eighth of this total (£2875.86). Milk traffic from Bellingham to Tyneside was of reasonable proportion. Station passenger receipts for the years 1874–5, and 1899–1900 (1 August–31 July periods) were as below:

Station	1875 £	1900 £
Hexham (NB)	1344	1386
Wall	190	164
Chollerford	823	1083
Chollerton	323	421
Barrasford	394	470
Wark	976	1023
Reedsmouth	683	453
Bellingham	1338	1612
Tarset	401	519
Thorneyburn	6	74
Falstone	372	366

Station	1875 £	1900 £
Plashetts	458	278
Kielder	284	250
Deadwater	64	60
Saughtree	127	77
Riccarton	638	256

Staff and the Weather

The BCR gave employment to men (and a few women at times) particularly at Reedsmouth, which with its sidings, important signal box, locomotive shed and associated permanent way staff, had employed several dozen, seven of whom in 1875 were for the station alone. At this date, Wark and Bellingham had three permanent staff, and the other stations usually one (excluding signalmen). Riccarton station had fourteen in that year. At this remote spot a school, church and club facilities developed to give the railway community facilities it needed. In 1875 there were six goods clerks on the NB at Newcastle Forth, reflecting goods traffic there. Occasional heavy snowfalls in winter brought out a snowplough attachment to a locomotive from Riccarton, but there were years when traffic was suspended for several days because of blockage. The exposed section around the hillsides from Deadwater to Riccarton facing a south-westerly blast up Liddesdale, was normally worst affected.

CHAPTER 5

The Hexham & Allendale Railway

Inception

Of all the branch lines built from the N & CR line, none was perhaps less probable than the Hexham & Allendale Railway. In all likelihood this line never was to make a profit on its operations. The fact that it was built at all is probably due to the determination of one man, Thomas J. Bewicke, manager of the Beaumont Lead Company.

The idea behind the line was simple. For thirty years the lead mines of the Allendale district had had to send their lead by cart or packhorse to the nearest railhead, chiefly the N & CR at Haydon Bridge station. This relatively short carriage to the railway was enough to increase expenses significantly, a fact which the lead operators recognised. The N & CR had considered a branch to Allendale Town and Allenheads in the 1840s, to serve the lead industry, but nothing had come of this. Alston had been the greater priority. By 1860, the irritation of the land cartage for Allendale lead was being added to by growing competition from imported lead, and there was a need to keep home-produced expenses as low as possible. The Beaumont Lead Company, under Mr W.B. Beaumont, considered that a branch railway off the N & CR into the Allendale district could reduce the company's costs and so help its general health. Beaumont's manager, T.J. Bewicke, actively supported the plan, and with his chief's authority, began to canvass local support for the railway. Support was forthcoming from the greatest local landowner, the Greenwich Hospital Estate, and by the other major lead concern, the London Lead Company. The latter owned the Langley lead smelter, south of Haydon Bridge, and $2\frac{1}{2}$ miles by road from the railway. Any line must therefore serve Langley smelter en route into Allendale. At Allendale and Allenheads were Beaumont's smelters.

Bewicke approached the N & CR, but because of the amalgamation affair, the time was not opportune. By 1862 this was settled, and his approach to the North Eastern Railway received a cautious but quite pleasing response. The NER told him that if there was considerable local support it would itself provide £10,000 towards a railway. Bewicke's fervour increased.

A route for a suitable line was surveyed, much of the course being over Greenwich Hospital lands in the Langley region. A Bill was prepared and presented to Parliament and found little opposition. Since it had great local support from the powerful estates and lead companies, down to the local population, there was not much could be said against it. It received the Royal Assent on 19 June 1865 (*28–9 Vic c87*). The Act divided the scheme into two sections with regard to capital. The 13 miles from a junction with the N & CR just over a mile west of Hexham and beyond Border Counties junction, to Allendale Town, was to have a total capital of £100,000 (£75,000 of which was to be raised by shares). The seven miles from Allendale Town to Allenheads was to have a total capital allowed of £60,000. The intention was to concentrate building on the first section, before embarking on the southern extension. As promised, the NER subscribed £10,000, and a similar amount came direct from the London Lead Company.

Bewicke advertised for tenders to build the line, on 4 July 1865: "Plans, Sections and Specifications may be seen from the 10th to the 15th July inclusive, at the office of Mr J.T. NAYLOR, 10 West Clayton Street, Newcastle-upon-Tyne. The Directors do not bind themselves to accept the lowest or any Tender." The Hexham & Allendale Railway Company was about to start its interesting career.

Bewicke's Line

The H & A was to be basically single track, climbing at a steep 1 in 40 from Hexham junction up to Langley, on the steep south bank of the South Tyne. From near Langley there was a gradual descent at first, then steepening to 1 in 50, to reach Allendale Town. The measure of the gradient up the Tyne banks can be judged from the fact that the junction was at about 150ft above sea level, whilst Langley was over 800ft. There were no great physical obstacles and few bridges of any note. Thomas J. Bewicke himself took on the capacity of "engineer-in-chief" and supervised the contractors. Mr Edward Brown of Newcastle was made Bewicke's resident engineer. Mr William Ritson was contractor. Money was by no means over-abundant, however. The small local population (6401 in Allendale parish) was not enough to give much financial support, but at first the finances do not seem to have been worrying. Bewicke's dream was the railway, and he instructed Ritson to build the works substantially; bridges would be of stone, abundant in the area. Since the major aim was to serve the lead industry, the first need was to get the way and rails in place. A passenger service was intended, but erection of stations and platforms would come only when the permanent way was finished completely.

By next year, the money problem became apparent. Bewicke went to Parliament and a second Act was obtained on 11 June 1866 (*29–30 Vic c78*) to allow the NER to subscribe another £10,000 to the H & A Railway Company. The support by NER is very interesting, when one realises that even if the line were not built, the NER still got the lead traffic. One may possibly put it down to the NER's desire to serve the districts in which it operated to the best advantage of those districts.

In December 1866 Bewicke was ready to give more of his time to his railway. On 1 December he was given a presentation on his retirement as engineer to the mines of W.B. Beaumont, MP "after 20 years' faithful service". He received a "very handsome tea and coffee service with a purse of £400 from Mr Beaumont, and a magnificent epergue claret jug and a pair of fruit dishes all in silver, from the officials, workmen and c. connected with the mines". The presentation was at the Miners' Room, Allenheads.

Early in 1867 when the formation of the first section was nearly ready, Bewicke approached the NER to ask whether the company would operate traffic on the H & A. The NER agreed, provided that the H & A paid for the costs of all rolling stock and locomotives used on its line, and paid the wages of all NER employees engaged in traffic on the line. On 15 August an agreement was signed whereby the NER received 40% of the gross earnings.

On 19 August the H & A was opened for goods between Hexham and Langley, with an intermediate station at Elrington. Langley lead smelter at last had a railway. The long-established lead ore traffic from Alston to Langley could now go all the way by rail; the refined lead could go off to Tyneside and elsewhere easily; Tyneside high-grade coal could be brought in to the smelter quickly. Previously much use had been made of the poor quality coal from nearby Stublick colliery, as the overland haul of coal from Haydon Bridge had been as expensive as the cartage of lead or lead ore.

The NER normally used locomotives based at Hexham on the H & A, and the H & A company paid for the use of the 1¼ miles of NER line into Hexham station. It also paid for the use of Hexham station for its traffic. The cost of a locomotive on the H & A was three guineas (£3.15) per day, and the H & A paid the crews' wages, any locomotive repairs, and stores used. A scale of rates existed from H & A stations to N & CR stations (east and west of Hexham). On the H & A itself, lead, lead ore, coal and lime traffic was charged at 7d (3p) per ton; stone, bricks, tiles at 9d (4p) per ton; general goods and timber 1s 0d (5p) per ton; and livestock 1s 6d (8p) per wagon. For through traffic in coal a minimum rate of 1s 0d (5p) per ton was charged. Through mineral traffic had a 9d (4p) per ton minimum charge.

On 13 January 1868 the remainder of the first section of the H & A from Langley to Allendale Town was opened for goods traffic. It included an intermediate station at Staward, which was the railhead for the West Allen valley. The station at Allendale was actually ¾-mile north of the town, near the village of Catton, and was named "Catton Road" up to 1898. The lead traffic from the Beaumont mines and smelters in the East Allen valley now had a much nearer railhead than ever before, lowering the distance by road for the lead traffic. In fact by now H & A finances were very low and the prospect of building the Allenheads section was already remote. During 1868 the company asked the Board of Trade to extend the time limit for completing the work by two years. This was granted. It mattered little in the event. Work was now concentrated upon erecting passenger station facilities.

Opening for Passenger Traffic

Bewicke and Ritson managed to get the stations at Elrington, Langley, Staward and Catton Road into order for passengers by early 1869. Each station except Elrington had two platforms, although one was for goods and parcels traffic only. The station at Elrington only had the single platform, and its goods siding was separate, but here and at the other intermediate stations there was a passing loop. The H & A station buildings were of wooden construction, with large brick or stone station houses. At Elrington the station house included the booking office etc, instead of there being separate buildings.

On 25 February 1869 Colonel Yolland, the Board of Trade Inspector, was conducted over the H & A by Bewicke, accompanied by Mr Henry Smiles of the NER (late N & CR) and Mr Milburn, inspector, and others of the H & A and NER. He was stated to have reported "most favourably thereon". The passenger service began on 1 March 1869. The *Newcastle Daily Journal* said that the service "will supply a want long felt by the inhabitants of the sequestered dales of the Allen, and will open out a new and picturesque district to the tourist". The initial service consisted of three trains daily on weekdays each way between Hexham and

103

Catton Road. Each passenger arrival between Hexham and the H & A paid a fare which provided the NER with a basic single rate of 3d (first-class), $1\frac{1}{2}$d (third-class). Return tickets provided other rates, eg second-class $3\frac{3}{8}$d to the NER.

Imminent Decline

The H & A was too late. By 1870 the lead mining industry was in steady decline, soon to accelerate. Depopulation of the Allendale valleys was already under way. Allendale parish's population fell from 6401 in 1861 to 5397 by 1871. In 1881 it was down to 4030. The collapse of the lead industry occurred from about 1880, most mines closing, and by 1886 the Allendale and Langley smelters had closed and the Beaumont lead concern had given-up its local interests entirely. This was catastrophic for the tiny railway; fortunately by now it was a minor branch of the NER. (One wonders, if he were still alive, at Mr Bewicke's thoughts.)

In 1870 the £75,000 share capital of the H & A had only been subscribed for to a total of £71,660. Only £6050 had been received in loans. In 1871 the £3340 balance of capital was issued at a 50% discount. The H & A received little return from its line, and soon envied the prosperity of its larger partner. Obviously, the directors and shareholders thought, "we will get a far better return if the line is part of the NER", but would the NER take over such a poor asset? In August 1872 tentative offers were made by the H & A to the NER, but the latter, not surprisingly, seemed happy with the existing arrangements. The H & A suffered in comparative silence for some time, watching the traffic decline and probably wondering why it had to suffer so.

Whatever the spur was is not known, but in late 1875 after further soundings from the H & A, the NER agreed to take over the line. On 4 February 1876 the NER directors reported that "an agreement has been made for the purchase of the Railway on payment of £60 in respect of each £100 paid up by the Proprietors". The H & A was wound up by the amalgamation Act of

The Newcastle area. *Above*: Ex-NBR Class D32 4–4–0 No 2448 approaches Blaydon with a train from Riccarton Junction, 1947, the engine in its last months in traffic. (*H. C. Casserley*). *Below*: Class B1 4–6–0 No 61012 *Puku* waits in Newcastle Central station with a Carlisle train on 12 September 1956. (*I. S. Carr*).

Hexham. *Above*: Class G5 0–4–4T No 67249 (NER No 1791) shunts a train from Newcastle in April 1952. (*H. C. Casserley*). *Below*: Class V2 2–6–2 No 60812 arrives with the 2.00pm from Carlisle in 1956. (*I. S. Carr*).

13 July 1876 (*39–40 Vic c102*) becoming one of the more rural, and certainly unprofitable branches of the NER.

A Quiet Rural Branch

The Allendale line was never anything but a sleepy by-way, passing through beautiful Northumbrian countryside.

In March 1879 the NER directors remarked that mixed or combined goods and passenger stock in same train on the H & A line saved £15 per week. The practice had been started in the early 1870s but ceased after complaints in 1875, only to resume after the hubbub died down. But the Board of Trade frowned on the practice, and the NER ceased such operations in 1880, despite the savings it made. The branch passenger service in 1880 comprised three daily trains each way (not Sundays), and a Tuesday extra each way (market day). The first train left Hexham at 7.55am, reaching Catton Road at 8.30am. Revellers in Hexham had to leave the town by the 5.55pm train or find other transport. All three intermediate stations were served by all trains. The fares between Hexham and Catton Road were 3s 4d (16½p) first-class, 2s 3d (11p) second-class, and 1s 1d (5½p) third-class. In 1887 the NER did some considerable first- and second-class fare-cutting, the new charges being 1s 11d (10p) first, and 1s 7d (8p) second, whilst third-class went up slightly. Connections to and from Allendale trains at Hexham varied, probably because the population served did not warrant much effort in providing good connections. Further, the decline of lead mining in the Allendale region, contributed to the fall in population of the area, from 5000 (1871) to 2000 (1911).

In the early 20th century, the service had improved to four trains each way, and two Saturday extras (reduced later to one). Noticeable in the H & A timetable was the long gap between a train at around 9.00am, and about 2.00pm. In 1913 the evening revellers on Saturday in Hexham, could catch the 7.55pm (SO) train back to Allendale. (Catton Road station was renamed Allendale on 1 May 1898.) Passenger receipts for the line were

£1700 in 1910; Allendale station had the greatest traffic, and Elrington the smallest.

Of other traffic types agricultural traffic, cattle, sheep and milk, was significant, Allendale being a dairying district, with sheep on the fells. Staward station, by a road near to the confluence of East and West Allen valleys, attracted much livestock traffic. A small timber traffic was usual at Staward and Langley, there being extensive local woodland.

The lead mining decline was marked in the 1880s. The West Allen mines closed in 1878, and the cheap lead imports into Britain forced the Blackett-Beaumont concern (which had been behind the H & A project) to give up mining in 1884. The London Lead Company also gave up operations in the region, selling the Langley smelter in 1882. The Langley Lead Company continued operating till closure about 1890. By 1896, only Allenheads smelter remained open, and by 1914 only one important mine, Sipton, near Allenheads, was still being worked. On the H & A lead traffic of about 1000 tons per year, in the early 1870s, sank rapidly in the 1880s, reaching about 100 tons of refined lead per year, or less, by 1900. Station results in 1900 were:

	Receipts £	Expenses £
Allendale	2246	171
Staward	769	94
Langley	512	62
Elrington	331	65

Very minor alterations were made to the line. Typical of these were the £70 spent on a goods loading dock at Staward in 1887, and £50 on enlarging Allendale station house in 1884. A linesman's cottage near the junction cost £250, in 1882. In October 1885 the NER reported that the flue bridge across the line at Langley was "in immediate need of repair". It took a fortnight to repair, during which time the smelt mill closed, and the NER paid £100 to the lead company in compensation. It seems a waste of money, as a few years later the smelter closed permanently.

The rolling stock in use on the line in 1910 was described by a writer as "superior stock for a branch line" consisting of elliptical-roofed two-bogie carriages lighted by electricity (and not the usual gas).

CHAPTER 6

The Tyneside Addition

Scotswood, Newburn & Wylam Railway & Dock Company

The early surveys for the N & CR had included a possible route on the north side of the Tyne through the industrial area of New-burn, before crossing the river. At the mid-19th century this area, just west of the growing industrial suburbs of Newcastle, was a populous industrial district, dominated by coal mining, with important glassworks, brickworks and other estab-lishments. There were over 4000 inhabitants of Newburn parish in 1851. To reach the railway, the inhabitants had to journey to Scotswood station, or go even further westwards to Wylam. It was inevitable that industrialists and local inhabitants would wish for a connection with the N & CR and undoubtedly there were many early requests, but the industrialists at least had the benefit of various wagonways carrying coal for pits down to the river, to staithes around Newburn.

In the 1860s, pressure grew for a more direct link with the N & CR. Industrialists saw all over Britain more railways infil-ling rail-less districts, even rural areas. A relatively short railway could serve the Newburn area. In the Parliamentary Notices for 23 November 1866 appeared the "Heddon-on-the-Wall and Ryton Railway". This stated: "Incorporation is sought for a company to make a railway from the Newcastle and Carlisle line near the Ryton Station, to a field in the parish of Heddon-on-the-Wall." Nothing came of this. By 1870, a course for a railway westwards from Scotswood had been surveyed, backed by the in-terested industrial parties. The line would meet several wagon-ways, which would join it, and use part of one (the Wylam

Wagonway) for its route. The only physical difficulty was a ridge of high land jutting towards the Tyne between Scotswood and Lemington, but this was not a serious obstacle. The promoters decided to include a new dock at Scotswood where local coal could be shipped, making (it was hoped) a small but highly profitable local railway and dock project. The scheme took on the title "The Scotswood, Newburn & Wylam Railway & Dock Company" and a Bill was prepared, presented to Parliament and passed without apparently great difficulty on 16 June 1871 (*34–5 Vic c48*). Parliamentary expenses were £3954 7s 10d (£3954.39). The railway, 6½ miles long, was to run from a junction with the NER Carlisle line at Scotswood, and rejoin the same line west of Wylam, crossing the Tyne at West Wylam. This western link was regarded as important, because the Newburn area pits were sending large quantities of coal and coke to Carlisle and West Cumberland. The dock would be reached by a short branch line, and was to be constructed in the low-lying meadows beside the meandering river west of Green's chain suspension road bridge and the NER railway bridge at Scotswood. In fact, the rather sluggish river and the obstacle to large vessels presented by the bridges seem to have been overlooked for possible difficulties, later to be recognised. The capital authorised for the whole scheme was £85,000 by shares and £28,300 by loans, which appears to be rather small.

The first sod was cut by the SNW chairman "in a field at Lemington under very favourable circumstances," during April 1872. The first contract for 2¼ miles of double track had been advertised on 19 February, the original tender contractor soon withdrawing, and the work awarded to George Bailey of Chester-le-Street at £26,542 13s 0d (£26,542.65). Work then proceeded on the Scotswood–Newburn section and borings were taken near Wylam to find the best site for a bridge over the Tyne. The line was to be double track because of "the probable extent of traffic", and all sidings were to be made "strictly to follow the practice of the N.E.R. Company on their Newcastle and Carlisle section". Probably the company already envisaged the NER

111

working their line, rather than the SNW having its own rolling stock. The Consett Iron Company supplied iron rails for the new line. By the end of June 1872, the sale of shares had brought in the sum of £23,300 13s 5d (£23,300.67).

At Scotswood, the projected cutting through the sandstone ridge soon met with difficulty. Bailey found that clay and sand in the strata were prone to slipping and a tunnel seemed advisable. It was agreed to build a ¼-mile-long tunnel.

On 9 May 1873 the second contract was let to the same contractors for the 3½ miles to Wylam village. Meanwhile enquiries were made of the Wylam Wood and Horsley Wood Coal companies as to whether their traffic might use the line. Whatever the outcome, the result was that the bridge was fixed for the most obvious site west of Wylam, and the SNW would cross the Tyne and join up with the N & CR line at Hagg Farm, West Wylam. Horsley Wood lay around a steep-sided meander of the river, and had the line been taken there, expenses would certainly have increased greatly. At the end of 1873 £38,710 9s 5d (£38,710.47) had been spent on construction work, and the line was nearly finished from Scotswood to Newburn. In September the directors had ridden in one of Bailey's wagons on a coal train from Throckley to Lemington ironworks. This run, on 19 September, was in fact the first earning of revenue by the SNW, as it continued to carry coal in the contractor's wagons when required. £54,283 8s 8d (£54,283.44) had been spent on the line altogether, at the end of the year. Scotswood tunnel was proving troublesome. The unstable strata were being held by brick linings, stone being used on the portals. It was still not finished in September 1874 when it partly collapsed, a bitter blow to the directors, as the line itself was ready to Newburn, but a link to the N & CR line had still not been effected. By now £80,000 had been spent on the line. The SNW sought a new contractor to rebuild and line the tunnel, which did not suggest confidence in Bailey. As the lowest tender received was as high as £2210 10s 10d (£2,210.54), Bailey was then told to make good the work.

Earlier, on 24 April 1874 tenders were advertised for the

112

Wylam bridge, whose design had been approved as a single-span wrought-iron structure. Hawks, Crawshay of Gateshead was to provide the ironwork (£9,380), and W. E. Jackson of Newcastle to add masonry work (£3,802).

At the end of 1874 in addition to £85,394 7s 8d (£85,394.38) spent on work, £10,000 had already been obtained by the SNW in loans, and capital was running dry. Then, over the winter, work on Wylam bridge was "greatly impeded by frequent heavy floods". The whole situation must have been very frustrating, with a single line of rails now ready from Newburn to Wylam, yet with difficulties at each extremity of the line.

By May 1875 the directors' state was such that they wrote to Bailey expressing their feelings, complaining of "the dilatory manner in which the works generally and the Scotswood Junction and works at Wylam especially, are being proceeded with". But in fact, matters were now resolving. On 12 July the line was officially opened from Scotswood to Newburn, although one imagines that the directors all viewed the tunnel with a certain degree of worry. Under agreement with the NER, the latter was to operate the SNW traffic and line generally. Passenger trains commenced between Newcastle Central station and Newburn with intermediate SNW stations at Scotswood (north of and linked with the N & CR station) and Lemington. There were 3 each way on weekdays. The NER was to maintain the line, appoint all staff, and operate traffic to its own requirements. Of course, the SNW had virtually no more capital, the dock scheme was virtually written-off already, and the line was a NER branch in fact, if not in name. Passenger receipts were to be halved between the companies but the SNW would take 70% of the goods traffic receipts. More complicated arrangements were negotiated for dividing the receipts on through goods traffic between NER and SNW. Examples of local (SNW) rates: minerals 1s 3d (6p) per ton, bricks 2s 8d (14p) for one ton, 2s 3d (11p) per ton for two tons and over, and general goods at 4s 2d–5s 0d (21–25p) per ton. On through traffic, the SNW would get, per ton, 4½d (1½p) on minerals, 7½d (3p) on bricks, 1s (5p) on general goods.

Dock Abandoned

At the end of June 1875, £104,601 3s 3d (£104,601.16) had been expended upon the line and £7951 on the new bridge. A special meeting of the shareholders on 9 September 1875 discussed the dock project, and concurred with the directors' recommendation that it be abandoned, a Bill to be obtained for the purpose. The Bill was rapidly drawn up and presented, becoming law on 7 April 1876 (*39–40 Vic c7*). It stated: "And whereas the construction of the said Dock has become useless by reason of the River Tyne not having been dredged upwards to such distance as to allow access thereto. And no lands having been purchased or contracted for the purposes of the said Dock or of the said Railway . . . it is expedient that the construction of the said Dock and of Railway to communicate therewith, be abandoned." The directors seized the opportunity of trying to get more money, as the Act also provided the SNW to raise more money to complete their works—£50,000 by shares and £16,300 by loans.

In early 1876 the NER examined the almost-finished Wylam bridge, and suggested modifications. As the SNW was hardly in much of a position to object to reasonable changes it agreed, provided that the NER paid for them. It was then agreed to have a joint ownership of the bridge, the Wylam Bridge Company being formed, both railways being partners.

Opening to Wylam

On 13 May 1876 the Newburn–Wylam village section was officially opened, there being only the one new station in Wylam itself (to be known as North Wylam station to differentiate it from the N & CR station across the River Tyne). The passenger services were extended from Newburn, and in the second half of the year passenger traffic increased by 16%. It is noteworthy that a second line of rails was not yet laid to North Wylam when the line was opened, although this was soon to be completed. This length of line was fairly level, and used a stretch of the old

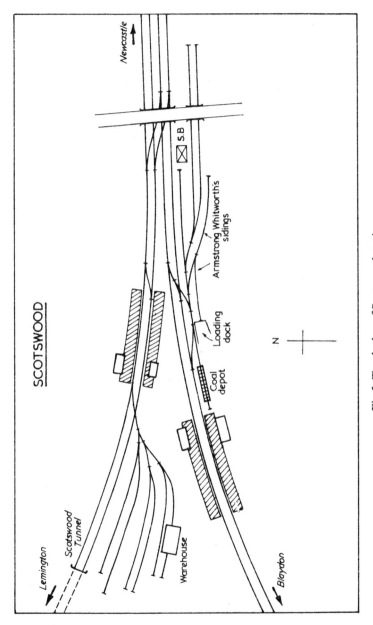

SCOTSWOOD

Newcastle

S.B

Armstrong Whitworth's sidings

Loading dock

Coal depot

N

Lemington

Scotswood Tunnel

Warehouse

Blaydon

Fig 5 Track plan of Scotswood station

Wylam wagonway for much of its route. It also passed beside George Stephenson's house of birth, east of Wylam, a fact which may have given more aesthetic satisfaction to the SNW if the harassed directors had any sentiment left. The SNW stations were not architecturally attractive at all. Two platforms were provided, with much use of the local red or cream bricks for buildings and houses. Footbridges linked the platforms.

The opening was recorded at length in the *Newcastle Daily Journal* of 15 May. The reporter produced the following account of his trip:

> The whole line is one of the prettiest in the Kingdom, running through one of the most charming portions of the beautiful valley of the Tyne. Immediately after entering upon it at the east end, we come to Denton Burn where there is a delightful glade which will afford an inexhaustable source of enjoyment to picnic parties and pleasure seekers in search of quiet-recreation from the toil and bustle of a town's life. Further westward we come to Sugley Dene and next to even a finer sylvan spot in Walbottle Dene, which with Denton Dene runs far into the country in a northerly direction. At Heddon is the old Manor House, which used to be the summer residence of the Monks belonging to the Priory at Tynemouth. About a mile and a half further westward we come to Street House, the cottage in which George Stephenson was born, and which will be one of the points upon the line most visited by tourists and pleasure parties. We also get a fine view of Close House, the beautiful residence of Calverley Bewicke, Esq. A portion of the line runs through a purely agricultural district, while at other points are industrial works, such as the steel works of Messrs Spencer at Newburn, and Messrs Grace's paper manufactury at Scotswood, and there are also collieries including the Walbottle, Wylam, Throckley, Montague and Heddon. The original waggonway upon which Stephenson used his first iron horse runs from some distance alongside of the line with which it might easily and with advantage, have been incorporated.

On that day, Saturday 13 May, an official opening and inspection train left Central station at 8.20am. Among the party was Mr William Cockburn, SNW secretary, Hubert Laws, SNW engineer, Godfrey Smith, NER Northern District passenger superintendent, and Mr George Bailey. Apparently many passengers joined this first train at the stations en route, and there were "large numbers of persons assembled" to watch it.

The typical newspaper comment on the new line could be repeated for so many 19th century railways.

> The line will not only be a great boon to the inhabitants of the district by putting them upon a level with other communities in respect to railway facilities, but will also open out to the inhabitants of Newcastle and the neighbourhood, a delightful district which will rapidly become a favourite place of residence, and will also afford scope for a further development of industrial works.

The line was equipped with Saxby & Farmer's "most approved system of signals", and the block telegraph system. Signal boxes such as that at Newburn station, which also controlled a road crossing near the station, were of red brick to NER design. The *Journal* reporter also mentioned that the "superior system adapted for laying the chairs and rails, makes the railway extremely smooth and pleasant to travel upon".

Wylam Bridge

On 6 October 1876 the most attractive bridge at West Wylam was opened, after an inspection by Col C. S. Hutchinson of the Board of Trade. Hutchinson's tests of the structure were very thorough, possibly because the design of the bridge was somewhat novel. The NER presence included Alfred Harrison, Northern Division resident engineer, and J. A. Haswell, assistant locomotive superintendent; the engineers of the bridge, W. J. & H. Laws of Newcastle, also attended. On the first test Hutchinson ran a locomotive of 36 tons plus 25-ton tender on the down line in the centre of the bridge—"with this weight little deflection was apparent". Then in a second test, the same locomotive plus tender and a 45-ton heavy tank locomotive were run on to the bridge. This was followed by 6 locomotives and tenders (weight 350 tons) coupled-up, run over the bridge on the down line "at a pretty good speed" several times. "Little or no deflection observed." A few more such tests were made. "At the conclusion of the testing the officials of the railway company were so satisfied with the bravery and daring displayed by the engine drivers and firemen (who are in the employment of the NER Company) who had been engaged in the work of testing, and with the courageous manner in which they had performed their duty in the face of the danger which had been apprehended by many, that they were invited to a dinner in the evening at the Turf Hotel, Collingwood St, Newcastle."

The bridge was one of the first built embodying the principle of an arch rising high above a road-bed, with the bridge floor suspended from it by vertical ties. The one span was 240ft 0in long. As Tomlinson wrote: "The beautiful little wrought-iron bridge over the Tyne at West Wylam was officially inspected on the 6th of October. Designed by Mr William George Laws, . . . it presented the appearance of lightness and grace rather than strength, but nevertheless came satisfactorily out of the unusually severe tests to which it was subjected. The cost of the bridge was £16,000." Col Hutchinson seemed pleased. "The admirable workmanship of the bridge attracted the marked attention of the Government Inspector, and he expressed admiration for it in the most unmistakeable manner." Less than $1\frac{1}{2}$ years later, Major-General (as he had become) Hutchinson was to inspect the infinitely larger Tay bridge which was not, unlike Wylam bridge, to exist for over a century.

Traffic

The passenger service from Newcastle was not extended over the new bridge. Persons wishing to travel westwards had to walk over the road bridge across the Tyne to the N & CR station, a fact which often led to local demands for through trains via the West Wylam bridge, especially when the NER fully took over the SNW. Thus NER records for 5 December 1889 note that Mr C. J. Bates of Heddon had "complained of the inconvenience for passengers on the Scotswood Newburn & Wylam line travelling west of North Wylam and having to proceed with their luggage from one station to the other at Wylam, suggests branch trains be run to and from Prudhoe. Resolved—the application be declined."

In fact, as far back as January 1877 a plan had been proposed to provide a new platform and sidings at Prudhoe station "in connection with Trains running on the Scotswood, Newburn & Wylam Railway, estimated to cost £815", and the NER had resolved "that the works be carried out accordingly". Then in 1883–4, the station was further improved. So the reluctance to make use of Prudhoe as the SNW passenger terminal is even harder to understand.

Special trains or excursions used the whole line when necessary, and it was a diversion should the line through Blaydon be blocked for any reason. However, goods services, and particularly the coal trains fron Newburn to Carlisle, used Wylam bridge. There was indeed, in the latter decades of the century, a very thriving coal industry in the area. Nearly £7000 came to the NER from local coal receipts in 1889. In the first half year of 1883, the SNW line receipts from traffic were as follows:

Passenger receipts	£589 13s 4d	(£589.67)
Mineral receipts	£1088 6s 1d	(£1088.30)
Goods receipts	£822 6s 6d	(£822.32½)
Parcel receipts	£34 15s 1d	(£34.75)

Besides coal and coke, bricks, iron and steel, scrap metal, clay and fireclay, sand and gravel, all were important traffic commodities on the line. "Rubble stone" from a quarry at Heddon was significant; over 10,000 tons a year were being carried in the early 1900s; the rate for this gravel was 1s 6d per ton (7½p) up to 1880, and 9d (4p) thereafter. Lemington iron and steel works also produced heavy traffic. Market gardening around Heddon produced a small steady traffic for Tyneside, but greater was the milk traffic at North Wylam. Of the local collieries, Throckley, Walbottle and Heddon gave the greatest traffic at this period. In 1894 the NER carried 43,378 tons 16 cwt from Walbottle Colliery (receipts £1849.71), 29,810 tons 9 cwt from Heddon Colliery (receipts £940.01). In that year, Walbottle sent 1500 tons of coal to Carlisle, and 1000 tons to Hexham, for sale to the North British Railway. Bricks were an important traffic, especially at Lemington, and the NER took 16,265 tons from here in 1906. Another 5875 tons were handled at Newburn. In 1880, a Saturdays-only train each way had been added to the then existing passenger trains each way.

End of the SNW Company

Although the traffic on the new line was satisfactory and generally rising, the SNW shareholders derived little real benefit from it, as the line itself was so relatively small, and the NER took a proportion of the income anyway. Like so many other minor British railway concerns salvation, or in hard facts, money, was seen to be possible in joining the very large prosperous company. Very soon the SNW directors, backed by their shareholders, were exploring this course of action. The NER would not be acquiring a useless asset in view of the line's traffic potential. On 24 January 1882 the NER stated to its own shareholders that it wished to take control of the SNW: "It is proposed to acquire this undertaking and to issue in payment for the same the sum of £35,080, in 4% Preference Stock, and £85,000 in Preference Stock, being interest for the first two years at 1% per annum, for the next two years at 2% per annum, for the succeeding two years at 3% per annum and thence forward at $3\frac{1}{2}$% per annum in perpetuity."

The NER took-over the SNW by the Act of 29 June 1883 (*46–47 Vic c63*), the SNW company being dissolved. Thenceforth the line was just another NER branch on Tyneside, but not at all insignificant, despite its relatively short length.

Changes at Heddon and Scotswood

The small historic village of Heddon-on-the-Wall, as its name suggests, lay beside the Roman wall, on the valley side high above the SNW line. A number of requests to the company for a railway station had been made, but it was felt at first that traffic would not warrant the expense of providing such a station. After more requests in 1877, the SNW inspected the line for a site in October, and an estimate of £750 was made for a station. Building began in 1878, but progress was extremely slow, possibly SNW finances being to blame. Opening day was 15 May 1881, and the cost was only £527 14s 7d (£527.73). Primitive wooden buildings were provided, and the site was 400yd from the river, but over a mile from the village itself, reached by a narrow lane climbing several hundred feet up the Tyne valley slope.

On 17 October 1879, Scotswood station buildings were destroyed by a serious fire. The signal box on one platform became the ticket office and performed other official functions until new buildings were erected. In March 1884 the NER finished new connections between the two Scotswood stations, with subways and staircases linking the various platforms, large wooden signs advising passengers which platforms to walk to for their destinations. New waiting rooms, road approaches and bridges were also erected and in the ex-N & CR goods station, new warehouses and sidings were provided. £5400 was spent on this work. There were nearly 110,000 passengers using the Scotswood combined stations in 1885 compared with 30,000 at Newburn in that year.

Mainly Passengers, Coal and Bricks

Traffic was particularly good from the 1890s to the early 1900s but in 1904, when Newcastle Corporation opened an electric tram route to Scotswood, some traffic was lost. The 1899 passenger service had grown to eight weekday trains each way, with two down and one up extra on certain days. A Sunday service was soon added, giving two trains each way. By 1913 the weekday service had 12 down and 11 up trains, one each way being an "autocar". By this date, the tramway threat was very real as shown in the Appendix.

Station passenger traffic and receipts in 1906 were as follows:

121

Lemington	71,442	£1325
Newburn	98,019	£3175
Heddon	13,623	£420
N. Wylam	21,362	£851

Goods receipts in 1910 were approximately £1098 at Lemington, £25,374 at Newburn, £437 Heddon, and £605 North Wylam. Newburn, the busiest station, had total receipts of £30,072 in 1900 (expenses only £755). This station's goods traffic (not minerals) totalled 154,613 tons in 1907, very evenly divided between forwarded and received.

Bound for the Border. *Above*: Class D49 4–4–0 *The Rufford* with the 4.27pm Newcastle–Hawick train at Reedsmouth on 9 June 1956. (*I. S. Carr*). *Below*: Class D49 4–4–0 *The Percy* heads a down train at Reedsmouth. (*J. W. Armstrong*).

The Border Counties line – 1 *Above*: Saughtree station, 28 April 1952. (*H. C. Casserley*). *Below*: Chollerton station. (*I. S. Carr*).

CHAPTER 7

Newcastle & Carlisle Heyday

The Carlisle Section

The N & CR lines within the NER became known as the "Carlisle section", in due course to become part of the NER Northern Division. Changes made were generally gradual, apart from the most obvious needs, such as repainting and renumbering of rolling stock and other fittings, signalling changes and adoption of NER rules and practices. The N & CR company, as recounted, had never been able to achieve entry into Citadel joint station, Carlisle, but the NER was because of its prior agreement with the LNWR in particular soon able to run the N & CR passenger services into Citadel. By an agreement dated 14 May 1862, the NER was a tenant at Citadel. It paid £1000 per annum, plus a contribution to working expenses. The London Road station remained open for goods, and the adjacent locomotive sheds were also retained. A new NER double line approach to Citadel left the Canal Branch (Canal Branch junction) 30 chains west of London Road junction, the distance into Citadel being 49 chains, and the connection opened in 1864.

At the start of 1863 the trains on the Milton–Carlisle section began to run on the left instead of the right, signalling having been adjusted, but only on 7 March 1864 was the rest of the line so converted. NER tickets such as the "day return" (March 1863) and "weekend return" (July 1864) were introduced, and from 1864 through special trains could be run from places such as Sunderland and South Shields onto the ex-N & CR.

Anthony Hall, N & CR locomotive superintendent, left office in September 1862, and Edward Fletcher, the avuncular NER superintendent, showed his tact and sense in not bringing rapid changes to the line. Fletcher did not believe in wasting the company's money (even if the directors had allowed it) in rapid standardisation as the NER developed and absorbed smaller railways. Rolling stock fit to serve was allowed to serve till time dictated otherwise. In the 1860s there was very little change in the N & CR rolling stock, and only a handful of locomotives were retired (See Appendix). However, the now green-painted locomotives did gradually lose their names, naming not being NER practice, but even here Fletcher was careful not to demand it; it took many years for all the names to be removed and many lasted till the locomotives were withdrawn. In the period 1863–7 old N & CR locomotives Nos 6, 10, 13, 14, 22 and 30 were withdrawn. No 19, an 0–4–2, went into Gateshead works and was rebuilt as an NER Class 25 2–4–0. In 1869 No 33 was rebuilt at Gateshead as a Class 675 2–4–0, retaining the wheels and motion, returning to traffic in 1870. In the next two decades further locomotives were dealt with, often drastically. Only in the early 1870s were the first NER-built locomotives permanently allocated to ex-N & CR depots, including NER Nos 64, 176, 177, 181, 185, 207 and 693, the latter being a Class 686 2–4–0 (Beyer, Peacock 1870) for passenger trains. Its usual driver was T. Thompson and it went to Carlisle shed.

In 1869 the NER brought its various constituent parts, dating from the various important amalgamations, into closer unity, with the consolidation of stocks. "Carlisles" were a valuable stock not easily obtainable. The proposal eventually put forward was to allot stock in the following proportions for every £100 of the existing nominal amounts: (*main examples*) Berwick £100, York £98, Leeds £65, Carlisle £133, Darlington £136. The shareholders approved, and a Bill was passed on 12 May 1870. "North Eastern Consols" was the name of the consolidated stock, and the former N & CR shareholders had done very nicely in the arrangement.

Improving the Line

On the N & CR main line there was a certain amount of activity and several very important works in the first decade after the amalgamation. Bridges loomed large in the activity. In 1865–6 the old wooden structures over the South Tyne at Lipwood, and over the Allen nearby, were replaced by iron girder structures. Because of the poor condition of the old bridges, Messrs Lane were engaged to erect temporary wooden bridges whilst Head Ashby & Co built the permanent bridges nearby. The temporary bridges cost £824 13s 10d and £292 4s 5d although Lane's work cost another £266 9s 10d more than the tendered prices. The iron bridges cost £3126 and £1387 10s respectively, and the actual course of the line was slightly changed to utilise the new works. The temporary single-line wooden bridge over the Tyne at Scotswood also needed replacement, especially as its condition was none too sound. Plans to replace it with an iron girder bridge existed by 1867, but in 1869 Mr A. Harrison, the NER engineer, was ordered in June to "take steps for having the bridge examined immediately and additional supports put in should such be found necessary". In September the NER ordered fire insurance (it was a fire which had destroyed the old N & CR bridge) on the bridge to be renewed only for six months "when present Insurance expires". The bridge was replaced in 1870 by the 6-span iron girder bridge which cost some £20,000. The Tyne Improvement Commission had asked the NER to build "an opening bridge" to ease Tyne navigation, and also requested deep foundations and as few piers as possible. The NER accepted all requests except for an "opening" bridge. A cast-iron girder bridge was built over the river Caldew in Carlisle in a very short time. The tender of Lees & Graham for £597 10s was accepted on 2 August 1867 and the work was ready by January 1868, although it did cost an extra £16 12s. Not far away at St Nicholas crossing, an embankment with bridge was planned in 1867 by Thomas Nelson & Co for £1126. Here the LNWR crossed the N & CR Canal branch on the level, and hindered traffic. Unfortunately, for some reason, this work was not done, and in 1870 there was a very serious collision here (later described on p139).

Mr Bourne, Carlisle section architect, was hard at work in the 1860s on possible station improvements. Hexham especially was an urgent subject for improvement, and local voices were not silent on the matter. Not only a growing N & CR traffic but the Border Counties traffic and, later, Allendale traffic made the old N & CR station far too small, and indeed rather disgraceful for current conditions. In October 1862 the NER replied to a complaint, stating that "alterations at the Hexham station would be considered in due time". Bourne produced a plan in March 1867 for a better station, although it included buying more land, the whole cost being £8000. This was referred to the Board, and presumably did not meet with joy, for nothing had been forthcoming by 1869. This was too much, and the feelings of passengers at the pokey 1830s station can be visualised. The Hexham Local Board of Health wrote to the Board of Trade complaining of the condition of the station, and in February 1869 an Inspector was sent to report. Colonel Hutchinson's report at last made for action in the NER, and "Mr Harrison [chief divisional engineer] was requested to prepare a plan for improving this station with an estimate of the cost. . . ." Thus in mid-1869 a veritable army of NER station planners was at Hexham, and every facet of the station received scrutiny, even the locomotive depot. In May 1869 the plan of proposed alterations and additions at Hexham station again worked out at £8000. In June the engineering works were estimated at £2240, waiting rooms at £500, and it was agreed to buy over an acre of land from Mr Beaumont for £600. In December it was agreed to put in the foundations for a locomotive shed and a 42ft 0in turntable for £100. In December 1870 J. & W. Lowry's tender of £2142 18s 5d was accepted for the following works: additional office, £552 1s 1d; roof over platform £1061 2s 10d; locomotive shed £529 14s 5d. Much use was made of stone in all the new buildings, and by 1873, when all was finished, the cost was put at £6700, which may have pleased the NER.

Many other changes of varying importance took place, so a selection must be made here. In August 1868 Bourne's plans for alterations and improvements at Riding Mill station were estimated at £450, and already 15 perches of land had been bought for £50 there. The old N & CR station buildings were replaced by new mainly wooden structures (not the station house, of course). In 1874 further improvements were made. In 1867 Wylam down platform was ordered to be lengthened by 70yd for £200. In July 1871 Mr A. Harrison's plan for proposed alterations at Brampton (Milton) station was estimated at £1500; the plan was approved and work on "the passenger shed and platform to be proceeded with at once". (The station name was changed to Brampton on 1 August 1870, and to Brampton Junction in January 1885.) In June 1871 alterations at Corbridge station were approved (£250) and suggested alterations at Blaydon be subject to further plans and estimates for future consideration. In September 1872 a "platform shed" was ordered to be made at Blaydon for £585 5s, and in September 1873 Blaydon station platforms "to be concreted"—estimate £68. In January 1873 "block signal stations" were ordered "to be done" between Newcastle and Carlisle, and in April 1871 it was agreed to order a 5-ton travelling crane from Cowans, Sheldon & Co for the Carlisle line. Earlier, in May 1871, Alfred Harrison reported on his examination of the N & CR tunnels at Corbridge and Whitchester, and repairs were ordered as recommended. This work cost £1000 for Corbridge tunnel and £200 for the other one.

The growing mineral and goods traffic also necessitated improvements at many places, often just a warehouse, a crane or sidings. In January 1865, for example, two examples reflect mineral traffic. Prudhoe Colliery requested a link between its new wagonway and the NER. It was resolved by the NER "that this be allowed on condition that the Prudhoe Colliery Owners be at the expense of laying down the requisite sidings on their own land, and pay 7½% per annum on the cost of the points and signals to be provided by the Company, and also half the expenses of a pointsman at the junction. That a cottage be erected for the pointsman at the above junction." The estimate of cost was £180. "A small depot for Mr Dinning's lead ore" was ordered for Haydon Bridge at an estimated £20.

In October 1871 it was agreed to extend the platforms at London Road goods station for some £80, and Mr Prosser (the NER's chief architect) was to prepare a plan of "additional stabling there for two horses". In December 1872 additional sidings at Blaydon were ordered for an estimated £10,000, "a portion only to be done at present". These were to be lighted with gas at an estimated cost for fittings, etc of £90 12s. Blaydon was in fact becoming a very congested place, because the branch to Consett had opened in 1867; there was a considerable mineral traffic in particular in both directions between Blaydon and this line, which caused problems with the passenger traffic operations at the station. In later years, very extensive sidings were to be laid down, and a new locomotive depot built at this point. In January 1866, a goods warehouse (estimate £50) was ordered for Wetheral station, but much more important was that built at Forth Banks, Newcastle. The old N & CR goods terminus was developed by the NER, and a large new warehouse was opened in 1870. The *Newcastle Courant* in January 1866 carried this NER advertisement:

> To Builders and Iron founders. The Directors are prepared to receive tenders for the erection of a large goods warehouse at Forth Banks, Newcastle-upon-Tyne. Plans and Specifications may be seen on application to Mr Prosser, the Company's Architect, Newcastle, from 5th to 26th February 1866.

In October 1870, the question of fire insurance for the new edifice was considered; the NER decided "that no insurance be effected in the Building, but that Hydrants with water pipes be placed all round it", which in modern times, may seem a second-best solution. Over the years, siding accommodation at Forth was improved. Nearby, it was decided that the line into Central station should be widened, a difficult matter as it was on masonry arches with occasional iron bridges. Property in Orchard Street was required, the owner asking £1450, and Mr Irving was authorised to complete this purchase in May 1871. Two years later, it was decided to widen the iron-girder bridges on this section of line, over Water Street, Vale Street and Errington Street, and this cost over £5000. At the west end of Central station itself in 1871, extra lines, a carriage shed and a boundary wall were ordered, and ready the following year. In April 1873 the company agreed to provide office accommodation for the North British Railway at Forth, the estimated cost being £180. The old N & CR locomotive depot at Forth Banks did not flourish, however. In October 1870 Mr Prosser reported on the transference of "the old locomotive shops at Forth Banks to Gateshead, and re-erecting the same there as an extension of the Smith's shops at £1150". Rather an ignominious end for a locomotive shed, but better than demolition.

Painting of stations usually involved a contract for a whole line rather than separate stations, unless they were very large ones. For some reason, Haltwhistle received separate treatment with the acceptance of a tender for £39 6s 10d. in August 1868.

Water supply or an excess of it could pose problems and two locations deserve mention. At Haltwhistle, the South Tyne was prone to periodic flooding after heavy Pennine downpours, causing subsidence in the Alston Branch embankment in particular. In August 1867 the NER ordered "that a yearly acknowledgement of 10s 0d. be paid to the Lords of the Manor of Haltwhistle for the privilege of having weirs on the gravel bed near Haltwhistle station". Later, in 1884, £160 was spent on such a weir. The long steady rise in the line eastwards from Corby, mainly at 1 in 107 past How Mill through Cowran cutting, often required a banking engine to assist a heavy train (even up to fairly modern times). With steam locomotives an adequate water supply was needed and How Mill station, two-thirds of the way "up the bank", was a good spot to replenish thirsty locomotives. In August 1870 the water tank at Haydon Bridge was ordered to be sent to How Mill, and in November of the following year it was reported: "The water supply at Milton

131

having failed, resolved: that two water cranes be erected at How Mill at a cost of £84, capital, and that an estimate be proposed for providing a pumping engine at Haydon Bridge." At Milton, a very large capacity iron water tank was subsequently erected, as being at the "top of the bank", water facilities were obviously important here also. In December 1877 the Brampton Union Rural Sanitary Authority "having applied for permission to take a supply of water from Cowran Cut for adjacent villages, and a report thereon having been submitted by Mr A. Harrison recommending that this water be reserved for the Company's own purposes, Resolved: the Application of the Rural Board be declined."

Finally to church and cemetery. In July 1865 "The Revd S. Atkinson having applied to purchase a plot of land at Rose Hill as a site for a Wesleyan Chapel, Resolved: that Mr. Irving be instructed to see Mr Atkinson and offer him a site at 3s 0d per square yard." And in November 1869 "an application for a subscription towards the cost of a proposed new burial ground at Haydon Bridge was declined".

Agricultural Matters

Agricultural traffic, particularly cattle and sheep, had always been a feature on the N & CR. Two important Tynedale agricultural shows were held annually, at Hexham and Bellingham, the latter of course only involving NB rolling stock. These gave rise to a brief but very large extra traffic, in passengers as well as produce. In later years, an agricultural showground was established near Corbridge, which gave that station a busy time on show days. For the Tyneside Agricultural Society's annual show at Hexham on 6 August 1866, the society's Hon Secretary Mr W.E. Thomson of Dilston Haugh, Corbridge, advertised locally for several weeks before the day, "return tickets at greatly reduced fares on the Newcastle & Carlisle and Border Counties Railways".

In that same year there was an outbreak of "cattle plague",

and at a meeting of magistrates, landowners and farmers at Hexham, a resolution was passed on the "expediency of adopting some more stringent measures for the extinction of the plague in the district". Mr Reed of Humshaugh proposed "that this meeting recommends that the railway traffic be stopped" and this was seconded. However, a vote was held and the resolution was defeated by 100 votes to 5, showing that in all probability the idea of losing the benefit of railway transport, however briefly, was not one most people wished to countenance. Mr T.P. Dod of Anick Grange, Hexham, then proposed: "That the chairman be requested to write to the North Eastern and North British Railway Companies asking them to be particular in ordering their servants to disinfect and cleanse out all their trucks at Newcastle, and in doing so remarked upon the carelessness of railway companies." Mr Trotter in seconding the motion said "he had always found the NE Company most particular". The resolution was agreed.

Passenger Services' Expansion

An outline of the main passenger service to the end of the 19th century shows a steady growth of services, and of traffic, so that the level of traffic by 1900 was vast compared with 1862. Certain important links at the Carlisle end had also developed. At Newcastle, Central station was always regarded as a terminal, as there was no real operating sense in having regular through services from the N & CR to other places than Newcastle. Convenient NER links to north, east or south always existed.

By 1880, there were five trains each way on weekdays, and two trains similarly on Sundays. On the Newcastle–Hexham section, loosely to be considered the "commuter belt" in later parlance, there were another five trains each way and two more also on Sundays each way. In addition on this section there were three weekday NB trains each way. On Saturdays, Newcastle's market day, there were many extra trains provided, and some were only between Blaydon, Ryton or Wylam and Newcastle. In

133

addition, there was a Newcastle–Haltwhistle extra, one way. There were no expresses, most trains stopping at all stations. However, one weekday Newcastle–Hexham train called only at Blaydon. In later years, especially after World War I, the number of trains calling at only major stations to provide almost express services increased.

Of the "special" stations Mickley, near Prudhoe, was basically for the benefit of miners, nearby Mickley Colliery being very productive at the period. Blenkinsopp halt, dating from N & CR days, was closed in 1875. Naworth, for Naworth Castle, the Earl of Carlisle's home, was eventually up-rated to full station status in 1871.

A station was built at Head's Nook in about 1860, which was more convenient for the inhabitants of the village of Cumwhitton in particular. Goods traffic was not dealt with, and the station was unofficial until after 1870. In the very different urban environment of Elswick, the suburb of Newcastle between the city and Scotswood, industrialisation and housing development had developed rapidly in the mid-19th century years with engineering, collieries and Armstrong's ordnance factory. Requests for a station to serve this teeming suburb had often been made in the early 1870s, and in 1875 an estimate and plan was prepared for a station (£1347). But the NER felt Central station was so close to Elswick that a station was unnecessary for so short a distance. So the 34,642 inhabitants of Elswick in 1881 had to walk or use horses. In 1886 the NER relented, the station being built in 1888–9 by J. & W. Simpson of North Shields for £3500, and opened on 2 September 1889.

In 1890, the N & CR main line service (NER only) can be detailed. On weekdays the regular service had departures from Newcastle Central at 6.25am (Carlisle, all stations), 7.35am (Hexham, all stations), 9.50am (Carlisle, no stops at Greenhead, Low Row, Naworth, Scotby), 10.20am (Carlisle, stopping only at Blaydon and Hexham before Haltwhistle, then all stations), 12.45pm (Carlisle, all stations), 1.15pm (Wylam—all stations), 2.30pm (Hexham—all stations), 3.05pm (Carlisle—express to

Hexham, then all stations), 3.45pm (Haltwhistle, all stations), 4.45pm (Carlisle—all stations to Haltwhistle, then stopping only at Gilsland (Rose Hill was renamed Gilsland in April 1869), Brampton Jcn, Wetheral), 5.35pm (Hexham, all stations), 6.10pm (Hexham, all stations), 7.10pm (Carlisle, all stations), 9.00pm (Hexham, all stations), 10.15pm (Hexham, all stations). Additional westbound services were the 7.55pm from Brampton Jcn, all stations to Carlisle, 10.50am Fridays only, Newcastle–Hexham all stations, and 6.30pm Haltwhistle–Carlisle, all stations. Extras on Saturdays only, were four, all from Central, and all stations: 11.05am to Ryton, 2.00pm to Hexham, 3.30pm to Hexham and 8.00pm to Blaydon. As an indication of time, the 6.25am Newcastle–Carlisle reached Citadel at 9.05am. The 3.05pm Newcastle–Hexham express reached Hexham at 3.37pm; an all-stations train similarly took about 52 minutes.

Up trains (to Newcastle) on weekdays, from Carlisle, left at 6.20am (all stations), 7.55am (all stations), 9.30am (all stations to Hexham, then only stopping at Blaydon and Elswick), 10.10am (only stopping at Brampton Jcn, and Haltwhistle to Hexham, then all stations), 12.15pm (all stations), 2.00pm (all stations to Hexham, then stopping only at Blaydon and Elswick), 4.00pm (all stations), 6.15pm (all stations to Hexham, then only stops at Blaydon and Elswick), 9.40pm except Saturdays, all stations to Brampton Jcn (on Saturdays only to Low Row, no stop at Naworth). From Hexham to Newcastle there were further trains at the following times: 6.30am (all stations), 8.50am (all stations), 3.50pm (all stations), 5.00pm (Saturday only, all stations), 7.20pm (all stations), 8.03pm (all stations), 10.08pm (all stations). Two more trains, calling at all stations, left Wylam at 1.48pm, and from Blaydon 5.10pm.

The Sunday trains were two each way, all stations, leaving Carlisle at 7.00am and 6.00pm, and from Newcastle at 7.15am and 5.15pm. Apart from the Sabbath therefore, this was a good service on the N & CR, especially on the Newcastle–Hexham section, where there were also NB trains to add to the number.

Joined by the Midland

The Midland Railway Company's main line to Carlisle from Settle Junction, to carry the company's London–Scottish traffic, joined the N & CR at Petteril Bridge junction, just west of London Road goods junction. The MR line opened to goods on 2 August 1875, and for passenger services on 1 May 1876. Thus, for less than one mile, the Midland trains passed over the N & CR, using the NER curve into Citadel. To some extent, therefore, the smart Anglo-Scottish expresses of the MR leaving Carlisle over the N & CR offered a grander sight than the NER 'all-stations' to Newcastle. But the two companies were to have, overall, very amicable relations.

A NER advertisement on 21 August 1876 for the "Cumberland United Temperance Demonstration" at Armathwaite, informed the public that an excursion train would leave Newcastle for Armathwaite on 30 August at 6.00am (return fare, third-class 3s 6d) returning from Armathwaite at 5.30pm. Presumably a Midland locomotive was used from and to Carlisle.

An Interlude of Accidents

In the years up to 1900, there were quite a number of accidents on the N & CR, most rather trivial but a handful more serious. The 1870s, a decade notorious in Britain for serious railway accidents, was also a period when accidents were rather too many on the N & CR. Those serious (by N & CR standards) accidents, and a selection of interesting if less serious events, may be recounted.

First, a long-forgotten tragedy illustrating the danger of everyday railway operating to careless staff. On 25 November 1865:

on the old Newcastle & Carlisle railway on that part of the line between Swalwell and Newcastle [*sic*] a boy named Philip Peel employed on board a keel was endeavouring to jump on to a team of waggons going along the railway at a very rapid rate, when he stumbled and fell between the wheels of one of the laden waggons. The poor boy's legs were nearly severed from his body, and on being taken to the Newcastle Infirmary, amputation was deemed necessary and both legs amputated a little below the knees.

Whether he survived or not we do not know, but his life was ruined.

Another solitary sufferer, although this time a fatality, occurred on 9 February 1866, on a level-crossing 1½ miles out of Central station in Elswick. A party of men for Mr W. Armstrong & Company's Ordnance Works was going over the level-crossing near the works "when a train—in all likelihood the passenger train which leaves Newcastle for the west at 7 o'clock—had come up". Thomas Foggan, a 23-year-old draughtsman, was killed, "his face was completely severed in two places". The inquest jury wished "that there should be a proper signal, or a person placed in charge of the crossing, to prevent such accidents in future".

Not far away was another level crossing, between Scotswood Road and a works, the "Crooked Billet" level-crossing, near the inn of that name. This crossing was "responsible" for the deaths of at least two women, an interesting court case, and also for a sidelight on the NER board, not altogether creditable in this case. The first accident, on 28 August 1868, saw the wife of William Hopper, a foreman at Elswick engine works, run down and killed. Her husband brought an action against the NER "to recover compensation for the pecuniary loss he had sustained in consequence of his wife being killed". The hearing at Newcastle took place on 25–26 February 1869, the QCs being Mr Manisty for Hopper, Mr Davison for the NER. It was stated that Mrs Hopper was carrying her husband's supper to him at work, between 9.00pm and 10.00pm. "Just as she got through the wicket gate between Scotswood Road and the railway a train passed from Newcastle after which she began to cross over. At that moment a train coming from the west and which the poor woman had not seen, came up and knocked her down and killed her." On the part of the plaintiff, Mr Manisty pointed out that the woman could not see the train coming from the west until she stepped on to the line in front of it, as the cabin for the watchman obstructed her view. The watchman was not at the gate to stop her from stepping on to the line, and it was stated at that time a platelayer who worked about 12 hours a day at platelaying, acted as watchman at night. Since this occurrence, another man had been appointed watchman. Mr Manisty contended that the deceased lost her life through the negligence of the company. With reference to the amount of pecuniary loss sustained by Mr Hopper, it was proved that he had five children, their ages ranging from 18 months up to 9 years; the youngest child he had been obliged to put out to nurse, and had had to engage a housekeeper to attend to the house and children. Mr Davison contended that no negligence had been proved on the part of the defendants, and that the deceased had not taken proper caution, and so contributed to the accident. His Lordship having summed up the evidence, the jury returned a verdict for the plaintiff, damages £100. The jury recommended that the railway company should put a bridge over the railway at this crossing. The NER did not think further improvements were necessary. But on 6 November 1871 a girl named Margaret French was killed on the crossing by a train. On 17 November the NER's appropriate committee recommended a donation of £2 2s to Margaret's father. One is tempted to wonder: where was the watchman?

On 2 February 1870 there was a serious accident at Haltwhistle. Apparently some platelayers, contrary to regulations, had attached three bogies to a passenger train; after a short distance, the wheel of a bogie had broken and the vehicle was flung off the rails, three of the platelayers in it being killed and five injured. The NER found that a local permanent way inspector, William Rutherford, had permitted the practice in the area of attaching platelayers' bogies to passenger trains, and the man was summoned to York on 25 February. In the circumstances he was let off very lightly: "In consequence of his previous good character, the Committee decided to continue him in the Service, but he was reprimanded and cautioned to pay strict attention to the rules in future." The NER sent donations of £10 each to the dead men's widows.

Later in the year, on the night of 9 July there was a very bad accident indeed at Carlisle. 0–6–0 No 36 with 27 wagons, driven by a solitary fireman, passed signals at danger on the Canal Branch and ran over St Nicholas' crossing right through a passing up LNWR Scots express; six people were killed. The fireman and his driver had taken drinks at the London Road end of the branch, and the driver had let his fireman alone take the locomotive to Canal and bring back the wagons. The fireman had not seen the crossing distant (defective—lamp unlit), but the clear red for danger and the lights of the express "had not registered". The incident showed a laxity of discipline at London Road depot. In the various improvements at Carlisle in the 1873–7 period, the crossing was replaced by a bridge, built by the LNWR and carrying that company's main line.

The Gilsland Collision

Four deaths occurred in the collision in Sheath Bank cutting, $1\frac{3}{4}$ miles west of Gilsland, on 5 July 1872. A ballast train, with platelayers engaged in eating their dinners after hours of hard work, was being propelled backwards on the wrong line, and met an up mineral train headed by 0–6–0 No 396; although both train crews saw each other's train, the sharp curves (two reverse curves of 26 chains radius in the deep cutting) prevented them from avoiding impact. The view along the line was limited to 160–180yd. The *Newcastle Courant* headline on 12 July read: "Fearful accident on the Newcastle & Carlisle Railway". It stated: ". . . the two trains collided with a fearful smash, the sound of which was distinctly heard half a mile away. The force of the concussion was such that the two ends of the van and both of the trucks which followed immediately afterwards, was projected upon the embankment in a thousand pieces. . . ."

The ballast train driver, on seeing the other train, had shut-off

139

steam, reversed, whistled, then put on steam, but was still going quite quickly at impact. The guard and five ballast men sensibly jumped out before the collision; on the footplate the driver, John Nicholson of Gateshead, also departed hastily, but his fireman stayed with his hand on the brake, and was not hurt. The Carlisle–Mickley mineral train had managed to slow to only 3–4mph, and its crew also jumped clear. As Lt Col F.H. Rich reported for the Board of Trade on 7 August: "The engine of the mineral train was driven back some yards, the buffer castings were broken, and the hind wheels were knocked off the rails." The guards' van and one ballast wagon were "broken to pieces" and a second wagon badly damaged, two others being thrown off the rails. Unfortunately the three platelayers who did not jump out all died, a fourth died with a crushed skull when jumping, a fifth man had a broken arm, and another, David Adamson, had a dislocated ankle. A special engineering train soon arrived to clear the line. The cause appeared to be the usual confusion in such cases. It was reported that a signal at Denton crossing was against the ballast train, whilst half a mile west a signal was against the mineral train, and there was also at the same place a man with a hand signal to protect the ballast train. So the question of why this man let the mineral train proceed is odd. But also, if Denton crossing signal was at danger, why was the ballast train proceeding so swiftly just beyond it? The verdict was all-round lack of care, but as frequently stated by government inspectors in such cases, it was the rather carefree way such inherently dangerous practices as wrong-line running were carried out, that led to accidents.

In an age without radio or television, newspaper accounts on disasters were often very lurid. The *Newcastle Daily Journal* account of the "frightful accident" illustrates this, and gives further details. The bodies of the three men still lying in the shattered remains of the van "being literally pounded together in one shapeless mass". One man, Walter Skelton of Brampton, married with six children, had "his head completely torn from his body and the upper part of his body frightfully crushed and

The Border Counties line – 2 *Above*: Token exchange, Kielder. (*H. C. Casserley*). *Below*: Class K3 2–6–0 No 61879 enters Wark with the 4.32pm from Hawick on 14 August 1956. This was a Haymarket engine at this time. (*I. S. Carr*).

Alston and Allendale lines. *Above*: Former NER 0–4–4T No 67265 waits at
Alston station on 29 May 1953. The Alston line closed in 1976. (*R. B.
Parr*). *Below*: NER Class C (J21) No 65082 at Elrington, with brake vans.
(*Folk Train*).

mutilated". The line of rails was "twisted about in a most singular manner". Driver Hall of the mineral train "did not realise apparently that there would be a locomotive on the trackwork. A man with a warning board was 1000 yards west of the work, yet Hall drove too fast." Yet Hall's locomotive had almost stopped when the collision took place.

1878–9

Three accidents in these years may be briefly described. On 2 July 1878 a relief passenger train from Newcastle running ten minutes ahead of the regular 10.20am from Newcastle to Carlisle, in connection with Carlisle races, came to a stand at the Crown Street down home signals. The regular train in due course ran into it and 61 passengers complained of injury, but only one was seriously hurt. There was little damage to rolling stock, the rear two carriages and van of the relief train being damaged: their bodies shifted on their frames and buffers damaged.

Maj Gen Hutchinson reported on the collision on 12 July. His basic conclusion was: "Had the driver of the NE train been provided with an efficient continuous brake, he would no doubt have been able to stop his train in time to have prevented the collision." In the circumstances, it transpired that Driver George Wild of the regular train, with 39 years' service, all on the N & CR, "mistook the lowering of the Crown Street home signal which was visible by him for a few yards, when 340 yards away from it" when the arm was lowered for a locomotive in front of the relief train, to enter Citadel. This assumption was of course erroneous. He released the tender brake on the falling 1 in 230 grade, and so was unable to reduce speed when he saw the relief train at a stand 120yd away, although 100yd was at a rising 1 in 107. He should have remembered the relief train: "He seems to have erred greatly in judgement on the present occasion." A coincidence was that John Dobson, driver of the relief, not well acquainted with the N & CR, had a pilot driver named John Wild.

When the boiler of 0–6–0 No 787 blew up at Blaydon on 24 November 1878 whilst shunting, the crew by good fortune escaped injury despite a tremendous blast. Maj Gen Hutchinson, in his report on 29 January, found that the "explosion commenced at a horizontal flaw near the top of the lower middle plate on the righthand side of the boiler. The flaw extended nearly the whole breadth of the plate." The locomotive, built by R. Stephenson & Co in June 1872, had covered 198,929 miles, and had had major repairs in October 1877 to March 1878 when the boiler (working pressure 135lb/sq in) was re-tubed and tested up to 220lb/sq in. "No apparent blame to be attached to any of the Company's servants as having conduced towards the explosion", he concluded.

On 12 August 1879, a lamp in a third-class carriage of the 3.20pm Edinburgh–Newcastle NB train exploded whilst between Hexham and Corbridge. Several passengers were slightly cut by breaking glass but no claims for compensation were to be put into the NBR. Again Maj Gen Hutchinson was in the northeast investigating, and his report was published on 29 August. James Cuthill, stationmaster at Chollerford, had found the lamp in coach No 537 broken, and fragments of oil on the floor and seats, and a broken pane of glass when the train was at Chollerford, whence it left at 8.45pm. After the explosion, one mile west of Corbridge, an inspection at that station revealed the carriage in darkness, oil on the seats and floor, and a strong smell of paraffin oil. Some passengers complained of paraffin on their clothes. When the train reached Newcastle 25 minutes late, Guard Joseph Milburn reported the incident to Stationmaster Reid. Hutchinson discovered that porter Andrew Carstairs, only six weeks in NB service, did not know how to reload paraffin lamps. "He poured paraffin into globes of some roof lamps under the curious impression that this was the proper way to supply them with oil. On the paraffin becoming heated it probably evaporated, caught fire, and broke the two globes in question."

Collision at Forth

On 1 August 1887 there was a collision at Forth when a NB empty coaching stock train ran into the back of the 5.10pm Blaydon–Newcastle passenger train. Fifty passengers and two staff were injured, none seriously, but it was a serious matter, and once more it was Maj Gen Hutchinson who reported (30 September 1887).

The passenger train was running slowly between the up distant and up home signals at Forth Banks Junction, and the NB train was bringing empty carriages from Scotswood station to Newcastle to form the 6.00pm to Edinburgh via Riccarton. The passenger train, headed by a tank engine, had its last three vehicles damaged, and it was pushed forward so that it hit a goods train standing in front of it, derailing two wagons.

Hutchinson said the collision was

> mainly caused by want of caution on the part of Robert Bowman, the driver of the NB Company's empty train. Had Bowman been keeping a reasonably good look out ahead, he could hardly have failed to see the passenger train standing or moving slowly forward near Forth Banks Junction in ample time to have stopped short of it, considering the sharp rising gradient (1 in 96) which his train was ascending and the amount of brake power at his command. He had been supplied with the Appendix to the NER Working Timetable, and this mentioned Forth Goods–Forth Banks Junction line working not being absolute block. The fact of his not being well-acquainted with this part of line should have made him more cautious.

Bowman had 27 years' service with the NBR, 20 years as a driver. His fireman, Peter McDonald, 5 years with NBR, was a "complete stranger to the line—he was attending to the fire and injector as they approached Forth Banks Junction. He should have been keeping a look out ahead." The NER local train driver was John Young, a veteran of 36 years' service with the NER/N & CR. Surprisingly, on 26 January 1888 the NER stated that it had agreed with the NBR to "divide the amount paid as compensation for injuries received in the accident—$\frac{3}{4}$ NB and $\frac{1}{4}$ NER". This appears rather generous treatment by the NER.

The Stephenson Centenary

1881 saw the centenary of George Stephenson's birth, and there were a number of events, exhibitions and other celebrations held in Britain to mark this railway landmark. In Newcastle there was quite a number of celebrations held, but the chief event was perhaps the locomotive procession held on the old N & CR from Forth station, just west of Central station.

In June 1881 at Forth goods station, locomotives ancient and modern were assembled for the public's gaze. There were also model locomotives exhibited including one of Stockton & Darlington No 1 of 1825 lent by none other than Edward Fletcher of the NER, and one of *Rocket* lent by Mr G.R. Stephenson. Mr Mitford of the NER permanent way department at Central station had a collection of exhibits of rails and chairs on exhibition "to show improvements made in form and quality". The full-size locomotives as static exhibits were "decorated with evergreens with extremely good taste and present the appearance more of a shrubbery than of a machine room which really it is". They included Hetton Colliery's *Invicta*, Killingworth Colliery's *Billy*, *Locomotion* (1825), the *Dwarf*, and "an engine built in 1839 by Alfred Kitching" for the S & DR company.

Meanwhile, influenced by the celebrations, "with a view of creating as deep an interest as possible among railway servants in the centenary, of the great engineer, the Mayor of Newcastle (Alderman Angus) gave £10 to be divided among the drivers of the best decorated passenger engines leaving the Central station during the day". (First prize £5, Second £3, Third £2.) One of the contenders was NER No 288, driver John Gascoigne of Hexham. "This engine, which usually runs between Hexham and Newcastle, was very beautifully and appropriately decorated with evergreens, the latter being tastefully arranged along the top of the boiler in the form of the High Level Bridge, and in front and behind the engine, were hung a safety lamp and collier's pick." No 288 had much competition, especially from East Coast main line locomotives, and whether it won first prize has not been ascertained.

For the procession of locomotives in steam, the high spot of the proceedings, sixteen took part "under the direction of the NER represented by Messrs I.L. Bell, *FRS*, E. Fletcher, Alfred R.C. Harrison, John A. Haswell, and B.C. Browne. Mr Godfrey Smith, passenger superintendent, was placed in immediate command over the engines, and the whole of the arrangements for the procession were carried out by that gentleman." The 16 locomotives were coaled at Gateshead, and coupled together, marshalled in a previously fixed order and steamed into Central station "along the south platform to the west end of the station". The locomotives were:

NER	No	363	built Gateshead 1880. 2–4–0 Class 901
NER	No	1268	built Darlington 1881. 0–6–0
NER	No	1000	0–4–4 tank Class BTP. built 1880 at Gateshead
NER	No	1435	4 coupled "bogie passenger engine"
NER	No	484	0–6–0 express goods, built Gateshead
NER	No	628	0–6–0 goods, built Darlington
NBR	No	493	*Netherby* 4–4–0, built Cowlairs, Drummond design, 1879. Used on Waverly Route
NBR	No	103	*Montrose* 4-coupled tank. Drummond Cowlairs
MR	No	1521	2–4–0 Johnson design, 6ft 9in driving wheels. Built by Neilson
MR	No	1451	0–6–0 goods. Johnson. Recently built by R. Stephenson
LNWR	No	619	2–4–0, Webb design, Built Crewe, 1880. Named *Mabel* after George Stephenson's wife
LYR	No	653	W. Barton Wright design, 4–4–0. Built by Sharp, Stewart
LYR	No	253	6-coupled passenger tank, built by Kitson, Leeds
LYR	No	313	Horwich-built 0–6–0 goods, Wright design. "One of the most powerful engines in the procession"
GNR	No	664	P. Stirling "single". New, built Doncaster
LB & SCR	No	329	*Stephenson*. New, built Brighton, "single" by Stroudley

Also on view in the goods yard was LNWR No 16, a Grand Junction 1842 machine with 6ft 0in single driving wheels, based at Crewe, and used by Webb for special trains, such as his own or directors' specials. Also interesting was that Mr George Hughes, later to become better known, was the driver of Lancashire & Yorkshire No 253. NER No 1435 was driven by a Mr Usher, "one of the oldest Carlisle men, and on the 11th of the present month will have been 43 years in the service of the Company". *Mabel*, the brand-new LNWR exhibit, was of the Webb 6ft 6in wheel type, and was to last until 1926. *Stephenson*, the Brighton locomotive, "was used last week in working the special trains conveying the Prince of Wales and other Royal Distinguished visitors between Victoria Station and Epsom Downs". NER 628, built at North Road Works, was one of the oldest classes of locomotive built there.

The procession had been arranged to leave Central at 11.00am on 8 June, but this was changed to 8.15am. With hordes of spectators at Central and all along the line to Wylam, the engines travelled out to that station, and returned thence at noon. It was altogether, a very nice tribute to the memory of "Geordie" George Stephenson.

To the Great War

The railway heyday really ended with World War I, 1914–18, and this is, for the purposes of this book, taken as the division with the years of decline. Traffic of all types was flowing steadily on the N & CR, with coal a major commodity. In 1894, for example, the NER received the following receipts from handling coal and coke traffic from particular collieries in the area:

Location	Receipts (£)
Blaydon Coke Ovens	1072
Addison (near Blaydon)	4912
Clara Vale (near Ryton)	11,710
West Wylam	11,906
Prudhoe	2373
Mickley	9231

Blackett (Haltwhistle)	4329
Featherstone (Haltwhistle)	4495
Blenkinsopp (Greenhead)	6542
Kirkhouse (Brampton)	4094

Vast amounts were carried—64,684 tons from West Wylam, and 87,081 tons from Featherstone, in 1894. Livestock traffic was quite considerable, particularly for Carlisle and Forth. In 1896, head of livestock handled at stations where significant were 771,782 (Forth), 128,699 (Carlisle), 36,697 (Hexham) and 21,022 (Haydon Bridge).

Numbers of passengers booked at each station are listed:

Station	1895	1907
Elswick	159,600	125,278
Scotswood	144,462	86,077
Blaydon	215,951	269,520
Ryton	77,485	122,459
Wylam	38,035	42,793
Prudhoe	59,660	67,629
Mickley	826	5,070
Stocksfield	28,885	40,186
Riding Mill	20,193	23,351
Corbridge	56,072	67,591
Hexham	101,557	126,796
Fourstones	22,542	23,434
Haydon Bridge	27,672	32,597
Bardon Mill	15,910	17,111
Haltwhistle	51,825	69,490
Greenhead	16,537	21,865
Gilsland	18,223	20,710
Low Row	7,739	7,657
Naworth	6,055	4,524
Brampton Jcn	32,299	28,715
How Mill	11,863	14,779
Heads Nook	13,173	18,368
Wetheral	41,137	43,729
Scotby	25,340	32,217
Carlisle	137,500	152,659

NORTH EASTERN RAILWAY.

Pic-Nic and Sports at Wetheral.
Flower Show at Corby, near Wetheral.

On Monday, 4th August, 1913,

An Excursion Train will be run as under to

NAWORTH, BRAMPTON JUNCTION,

(For Talkin Tarn)

HOW MILL,
WETHERAL & CARLISLE

Fares there and back—
Third Class.

	A.M.	To Naworth and Brampton Junction	To How Mill Wetheral and Carlisle
Newcastle dep	**8 32**	**3/6**	**3/9**

Children not exceeding 3 years of age, free; above 3 and under 12 years of age, half–fare.

RETURN ARRANGEMENTS the same day, as follows :—

Carlisle ...	...	...	dep. 7	50 p.m.
Wetheral ...	...	...	,, 8	3 ,,
How Mill...	...	...	,, 8	13 ,,
Brampton Junction...	...	...	,, 8	24 ,,
Naworth ...	...	...	,, 8	30 ,,

CONDITIONS.

The tickets issued at the above fares are only available for the Excursion Train from and to the stations at and for which they are issued, and are not transferable, and no passenger will be allowed to leave or join the train at any intermediate station. Passengers travelling by this train without having first obtained a ticket for it will be required to pay the ordinary single fare.

The tickets are only available for those excursionists who travel by the Excursion Train on both outward and return journeys. Any person using the Excursion Train for the outward journey only, or for the return journey only, will be required to pay the ordinary fare for the journey taken, notwithstanding that such person is provided with an Excursion ticket.

This excursion is advertised and arranged by the Company subject to the general conditions and regulations specified in the current time tables, to which intending excursionists are referred.

A limited number of carriages will be provided for this Excursion, and intending passengers should apply early for tickets, which can now be obtained at the above mentioned Stations, and at Messrs. THOS. COOK & SON, General Railway and Steamship Agents, 2, Northumberland Street, Newcastle.

NO LUGGAGE ALLOWED.

Bicycles, Perambulators, and Mail Carts will be conveyed at the rate shewn in the Company's Time Tables.

For further information respecting this Excursion, apply to Mr. E. F. WILKINSON, District Passenger Agent, Newcastle.

H.N. 115—Howe Brothers, Printers, Melbourne Street, Gateshead.

Fig 6 Excursion handbill, 1913

Traffic was very good. The only disquieting feature was apparent in Newcastle, where the electric tramways to the suburbs (begun in 1901) especially for the N & CR, the Scotswood Road routes (and beyond to Lemington and area) were abstracting some passengers. For further traffic statistics and station receipts/expenses see Appendix 3. Appendix 6 gives information on the tramways in 1913.

The NER continued the old N & CR tradition of excursion trains. Gilsland (for the spa), Brampton, Alston, Hexham and Corbridge were popular places for Tyneside outings. The annual show of the Tyneside Agricultural Society at Hexham in each August normally saw many extra trains from Newcastle. The NBR also gave Tyneside outings up the Border Counties line to North Tynedale and Scotland.

In the 1890s, the NER reached an understanding with the Caledonian Railway for west coast Scottish traffic, significantly made when the NER was having "friction" with the North British, ancient enemy of the CR. A through Newcastle–Glasgow via Carlisle service using each company's rolling stock was started, the distance competing favourably with Newcastle–Glasgow via Edinburgh and need to change trains at least once. Later with better relations with the NB, the Caledonian link was discontinued.

Also begun and very long-lasting was a "small hours" express to and from Carlisle, in connection with the Portpatrick and Wigtownshire route to Stranraer and Ireland. In 1899 the boat train express to Carlisle left Newcastle at 1.10am. In the other direction, the boat train often called "The Paddy" left Carlisle at 12.05am. It took only 1½ hours on the N & CR, and this train was still running in the 1970s (although its Scottish route has changed).

In the period, further changes were made on the line in various ways. Some of the most important improvements were the widening to four tracks of the Scotswood–Elswick–Forth section, greatly helping to end the congestion there. Elswick station was made into an "island" with its faces to two running lines

only. Forth-Central station was widened in 1906. The mile-long
Eltringham river wall was greatly strengthened in 1914. Blaydon station was completely rebuilt and enlarged in 1911, a red-
brick structure replacing the old buildings. Gilsland was rebuilt
in 1905–6 in a very attractive fashion with a platform canopy on
the up line. H.M. Adamson writing in 1910 called it "one of the
most convenient and up-to-date on the whole section". Warden
bridge was replaced for the second time in 1906, with a steel
girder structure, again on a different site to the previous structure, requiring slight re-alignment. Also at Warden, and not previously mentioned, was a paper mill, old established and with its
own siding from the N & CR. This was (and still is) the South
Tyne Mill of the Fourstones Paper Mill Company. Blaydon's
new large locomotive depot was opened in April 1900, and
henceforth contributed much of the motive power used on the
N & CR and other lines.

Some Station Observations

Finally, Adamson's views on the N & CR in 1910, and a few
more of its stations, are worth quoting:

> Yet even today this section is operated almost as if it were a separate
> railway, for its train services although connecting with numerous to
> and from all parts of the country at each end, are to a great extent
> arranged on an independent basis owing to the fact that, while many
> and varied connections are made by each train, no particular con-
> nection is, as a rule, more important than another except in certain
> special cases.

Writing about Hexham station he said:

> The station is still very inconvenient and old-fashioned. The passen-
> ger station consists of two "through" platforms, the up and down
> respectively, the former having a bay for the Newcastle local trains,
> while the down platform has a very short bay for the Allendale
> trains, etc. The accommodation is ludicrously inadequate for when,

as is frequently necessary, slow trains have to shunt into this bay to allow expresses to pass, only one third of the train is alongside a platform at all! . . . Haydon Bridge station is a very old-fashioned erection, with practically no cover at all on the down platform, and only very limited shelter on the up platform, while there is no footbridge for connecting the platforms.

Red-brick station buildings had been erected there on the down platforms (where stone would have been more in character with the town). The pedestrian footbridge, of iron and sometimes with wooden shelter, was a feature of NER stations. Ryton had a subway, and at various dates, subways had been planned at Hexham and Brampton, but footbridges were made instead, in some cases, such as Hexham, covered footbridges. An interesting feature of some N & CR stations (which has lasted to the present day) was the rather low platform levels, never altered in height from N & CR company days.

Rolling Stock

Coaching stock improved over the years. In the mid-1870s, much was still "semi-open", and 6-wheelers. In May 1876 a man named John Rowland was charged at Newcastle Police Court with molesting a young woman in a train between Wylam and Newcastle on 7 April; he had "climbed over the partition separating the compartments" in a third-class carriage. Bogie carriages were commoner by 1914.

Locomotives also improved. The Class A 2–4–2T and Class BTP and O 0–4–4T were common on passenger trains, especially the Newcastle–Hexham locals. Classes 675, 686, 901 and 1440 2–4–0s saw much service, as did the McDonnell 4–4–0s of 1884. Later Worsdell 4–4–0s such as Class F also became common, but they did not oust the earlier types until the 1920s. For goods and mineral traffic many 0–6–0 classes could be found, and naturally the most numerous classes such as class 398 and the C, C1 classes and some of the P class family would be seen.

One must conclude this very brief section by mentioning what are believed to have been the last N & CR locomotives in use. In the 1880s the last survivors were disappearing, some being rebuilt to tank engines at Gateshead, for instance No 461 (ex-N & CR No 12) *Carlisle*, rebuilt to 0–6–0ST in 1881, and No 487 (ex-No 39) also to 0–6–0ST in July 1883. No 488 (ex-N & CR No 40) *Langley* was still at work on the Carlisle–Brampton section in 1879, based at London Road, and it has been said that this was probably the last N & CR locomotive in use unrebuilt. The North British types to be seen on the N & CR included various classes of 2–2–2, 0–6–0, 4–4–0, 4–4–0T and 4–4–2T in particular. The 2–2–2s with 4-wheel tenders were rebuilt Beyer-Peacock ex-Edinburgh & Glasgow Railway engines (1856–61 vintage), the last survivor being No 1006, withdrawn 1912. Certain heavier NBR classes such as the Atlantics were not able to use the Border Counties line, the Tyne Bridge at Hexham being none too strong, and so did not appear on the line.

CHAPTER 8

The Brampton Railway

The Earl of Carlisle's Line

Although some wooden wagonways existed on the Tindale Fells to serve the Earl of Carlisle's collieries before, it is generally accepted that 1798 marked the opening of the Earl's railway proper from Brampton town coal staithes to the Tindale mines. Thus the Earl's railway was in operation long before the Newcastle & Carlisle Railway was even thought of. It is not intended to give the full history of the Brampton Railway, of which much has been written elsewhere (eg *The Brampton Railway* by John N. Charters—Oakwood Press) but only to relate basic relationships with the N & CR.

In the early 1820s, the Brampton Railway was extended to serve new coal sinkings, at Midgeholme on the county boundary, and Blacksyke, south-east of Talkin Tarn. At Kirkhouse, between Milton and Hallbankgate, the offices, engineering works and other facilities (including coke ovens) were set up for the railway.

With the coming of the N & CR, it was realised that the Brampton line would cross the new line at an awkward point north of Milton village, and a revised course was planned, to take the Brampton on a more southerly course from Hallbankgate, to about ¾-mile south of Milton, connect with the N & CR there, before adopting another new course to Brampton town. George Stephenson, a friend of James Thompson, who was the Earl's agent in control of mines and railway, surveyed the revised Brampton course in 1835; construction quickly took place, the line opening on 8 July 1836. The line included an inclined plane

155

between Kirkhouse and Hallbankgate (grades up to 1 in 17½)
and a deep cutting at Rowbank Plantation, Milton.

The connection put in between the Brampton and the N & CR
at Milton allowed Tindale coal to travel to Carlisle all the way on
the N &CR if desired, instead of going to Brampton. There was a
formal opening ceremony on 13 July 1836, when a train of 23
wagons and carriages left Kirkhouse for Brampton hauled by the
Earl's locomotives, *Gilsland* and *Atlas*. Ten loaded coal wagons
were included. Apparently, a N & CR passenger coach *Emerald*
was part of the rolling stock. It is perhaps worth noting the fairly
amicable relationship from the start between the venerable
Brampton Railway and the new N &CR, no doubt helped by the
Earl of Carlisle's support for both.

The Dandy

James Thompson soon began organising a passenger service on
the Milton–Brampton section of the Brampton Railway, with an
eye on the population of the town of Brampton whose connection
to the N & CR was most quickly effected by his own line. A horse-
drawn "dandy" service was instituted, the horse pulling several
open carriages, replaced in 1839 by covered carriages with
names such as *Black Diamond*. The original fare was 3d (1p) .
Suffice to say, the operating conditions were not those which in
later years any Board of Trade inspector would have countenanced without apoplexy. The regular driver of the "Dandy",
from 1839 to 1881, was Mr George Mingins of Brampton. Over
the years of the mid-19th century, as the operation of British
railway companies advanced and improved generally, the primitive "Dandy" soon began to draw occasional demands from the
3500 good citizens of Brampton for more appropriate transport.
Eventually the Brampton and the North Eastern Railways were
to take notice. In the 1870s the NER records contain persistent
references to applications and memorials for some improved
passenger link for Brampton town. Meanwhile on 1 August
1870, Milton station had been officially re-named Brampton,

whereupon the inhabitants soon memorialised the NER in 1871 "Requesting that the NE Company should construct a branch line of railway from Milton Station (*sic*) into the Town of Brampton", the use of "Milton" sounding rather like pique. After deliberation, the NER response in August 1872 was: "The Directors do not feel justified in recommending the Shareholders to construct or subscribe towards the construction of any railway in the Brampton District at present, in consideration of the great increase in Railway expenses." In the same month all rates and fares on the NER had been raised by up to 10% due to increased costs of labour, fuel and materials. However, the use of the phrase "at present" was hardly calculated to muzzle the Bramptonians.

Modernisation—Steam at Last

In 1837 the Earl leased the BR, collieries etc., to James Thompson and his heirs, and ceased to have any direct interest in day-to-day affairs. Thompson died in 1851, and was succeeded by his son Thomas Charles (born 1832).

It must be understood that the Brampton Railway used steam locomotives on its coal trains, many being built at its Kirkhouse workshops. Why did the people of Brampton have to have a (slow) horse? Thompson & Sons' views on the matter have not apparently been recorded, but the Brampton Railway did borrow for one day, 13 November 1878, some NER carriages to convey passengers on the Brampton service. It is not reported what the passengers felt on seeing the horse again the next day! Meanwhile in March 1875 a deputation from Brampton met NER officials to talk about a branch railway. The NER ordered Mr Harrison its engineer to submit plans and sections, and he did so by August. In September a deputation from Brampton met the NER officers and were shown plans for two alternative branch lines into Brampton. The deputation stated that it would be satisfied if either were carried out. The directors then said they would communicate with Major Thompson before coming to a

157

decision. Thus, on 22 October it was reported curtly: "The Deputation to be informed that the Directors decline making a new line." There is something of a mystery about Thompson's attitude. Why could not he provide a steam locomotive and a couple of carriages? Apparently, on occasions such as the Brampton Show, such a service would be provided for a day.

The good citizens of Brampton must have been angry. In mid-1877 a Mr John Carrick asked for a reconsideration of the matter, and on 9 November was dustily told that the 1875 decision would be adhered to. This appears to have irritated Mr Carrick, for by May 1878 we find him complaining to the NER of the "insufficient height of the platforms at Brampton station", which is interesting in that at that very time the company was involved in improving the platforms as the result of complaints to the Board of Trade by a Dr Wotherspoon late the previous year. Brampton must have been a touchy name at the period in NER meetings.

However, improvements for Brampton were nigh. A local poet, Peter Burn, wrote a disparaging poem on the "Dandy" in 1880, the most biting verse being:

Full 40 years have had their run
I've had my share of work and fun
I've seen strange things beneath the sun
But nought to match the Dandy.

Major Thompson agreed to convert the passenger service to steam power, and use more modern carriages. Three ex-LNWR 4-wheeled carriages were bought, and the "coal staithes" station at Brampton town was improved and named Brampton Town. It had a single platform face. A new side tank 0–6–0 locomotive named *Dandie Dinmont* was bought from Neilson's of Glasgow, and the regular service began on 1 July 1881. Thus at last the people of Brampton had a reasonable passenger rail link to the NER. Brampton, (NER) ex-Milton station, became, unofficially, known as Brampton Junction (the name became official

Around Wylam. *Above*: Class BI 4–6–0 No 61219 crosses the Tyne at Wylam with a down train. (*J. W. Armstrong*). *Below*: George Stephenson's birthplace beside the SNW line. (*Author*).

Diesels arrive. *Above*: Brush Class 47 No 1942 on an eastbound tank wagon train at Bardon Mill on 21 December 1970. (*Author*). *Below*: Class 37 No 6917 heads an eastbound goods in Cowran Hills cutting on 7 January 1971. (*Author*).

from January 1885), a name which it retained even in 1977.

Thomas Thompson died in 1888, and his son Charles Lacy (born 1857) replaced him as head of Thompson & Sons.

A Blow for Brampton

In 1890 the Thompson lease required renewal, and the Earl of Carlisle stipulated that the Junction–Town line should be inspected by the Board of Trade. As the "Dandie Dinmont" line had very primitive operating conditions, eg no signalling, no continuous brake on a line reaching 1 in 30 grade, no locked facing points, etc, the Board of Trade advised several operating changes. Charles Thompson felt unwilling to go to the expenditure (despite the booming trade by the Thompson coal mines which must have provided much capital), and gave notice to withdraw the passenger service on 30 April 1890. This was done, *Dandie Dinmont* was sent to the coal traffic, and the townspeople of Brampton had to walk or be horse-borne to the Junction; the outcry was enormous. Petitions flooded into the NER, and the NER director (later deputy-chairman) Sir Lothian Bell MP was a channel of communication. Lord Carlisle offered to sell the line to the NER, and it is even believed he might have been willing to give it to the company for a nominal fee. It was by this time rarely used for coal or other traffic, most of the mineral traffic, coal and lime chiefly, leaving the Junction by the NER.

But the Bramptonians were left to their own devices this time, and Thompson soon had more pressing financial worries, such as the exhaustion of Midgeholme colliery, closed in 1893.

North Eastern Take-Over

In 1905 the vexed question of a passenger service for Brampton raised itself again above the usual rumblings, with the NER asking Sir Hugh Bell, the local MP, to ascertain Lord Carlisle's views. Negotiations between NER, the Earl, and Thompson & Sons began again. On 1 December 1905, under the heading

161

"Railway facilities at Brampton", The *Newcastle Daily Journal* stated the following:

> For some time past negotiations have been carried on with the North Eastern Railway Co with a view to getting improved facilities for passenger traffic between the town and Brampton Junction; a distance of two miles by way of the existing "dandy" line which has been offered by Lord Carlisle for the purpose. Various officials of the company have inspected the suggested routes but no definite reply has up to now been received. In reply to inquiries made by Mr Hugh Jackson, Chairman of the local light railway committee, two railway officials from York had an interview with Mr Jackson at his residence on Wednesday afternoon. Having explained the causes of the delay and reported upon the present position of the Scheme, Mr Jackson was authorised to make the following statement: That the question had received careful consideration by the NER Co and that, subject to satisfactory local arrangements being made, the railway company may consider favourably the proposal to work the existing line for passenger and other traffic. A movement is on foot to establish a service of motor 'buses between Brampton and Carlisle by road, but in view of the large number of excursionists who visit the town in summer, it is felt that facilities in the other direction are urgently needed.

Meanwhile the Thompson era ended suddenly. In 1908 after an accident at Roachburn colliery when three miners died, Charles Macy-Thompson's health gave way, and in May the business was dissolved. The lease passed to a consortium named the Naworth Coal Company, but the $1\frac{3}{4}$ miles between Brampton Junction and Town was not included, although it stayed open for coal to the Brampton depot.

The seemingly eternal talks between NER and Lord Carlisle continued, the former at one point threatening to break off the negotiations because of the "exorbitant" terms being asked. No progress was made until the Earl died in 1912, and the NER signed a 50-year leasing agreement with the Countess of Carlisle on 29 October 1912.

Some £900 was paid by the NER on permanent way improvements, the line (single track) was relaid, and there was a new goods warehouse constructed. The old stone bridge over the Brampton–Alston road (built in 1836) was replaced by a girder structure. A reasonable booking office, separate waiting room and a run-round loop for the branch engine were also built.

Celebration

The official opening ceremony was on 31 July 1913, with regular services to commence on 1 August. Much pomp and ceremony attended the ceremonial function. Even the NER chairman was present. Lady Cecilia Roberts, a daughter of the late Earl of Carlisle, performed the ceremony. The *Newcastle Journal* reported:

> The train, composed of an engine, No 1089 (BTP 0–4–4T dating from August 1877) and two carriages, was also decorated, and under the influence of brilliant sunshine, the old market town presented a decidedly festive appearance. Business had been suspended and a large crowd of residents and visitors participated in the proceedings. The town station is situated at the south east corner of the Sands, just where the old Dandy used to take up or set down its passengers. Lady Cecilia hoped that the railway would be a blessing to their beloved Brampton in every way (cheers). The first train shortly afterwards steamed out of the station amid enthusiastic cheering and the noise of fog detonators. When the party returned, there was a procession headed by a brass band from the station to the Howard Arms Hotel, where a public luncheon was held. Ald. Hugh Jackson (chairman of the Brampton Railway committee) presided.

Mr Jackson's reported speech:

> During the early stages of the railway system, the people of Brampton and neighbourhood like many other communities at that time, protested against railways coming near them, and they had often been reminded of that. For the last 40 years, efforts had been much to induce the NE Rly Co. to go to Brampton. The last successful attempt was started by the Parish Council 10 years ago. He felt that if the NER Company would see their way to carrying goods traffic over the new section it would tend to stimulate the starting of industries in the town.

Sir Walter Plummer, a director of the NER since 1905, stated: "It was up to them to show that the line would be a paying and prosperous line for the NER Company. They had 50 years to prove that the line could be a success, and he believed they would do it."

A Brief Success

Success was very brief indeed, but no one in 1913 knew what lay just ahead. By the end of 1913, 7564 passengers were carried on the branch (receipts £464), and in 1914 the figures were 14,706 passengers, £1026 receipts. In 1914 Brampton Town station receipts totalled £1325, expenses £159. Coal traffic on the branch was 4733 tons during 1913. The branch trains connected with east and west bound N & CR trains, and there was a short bay platform at the west end of Brampton Junction station. The "steam autocar" service, normally used on the branch passenger works, consisted of a BTP tank locomotive permanently coupled to a coach at each end.

On the mineral front, the rest of the old Brampton Railway continued to produce coal and lime at the Junction station, and from 1908 this was the only rail outlet, as the Midgeholme–Lambley section (connecting thus with the Alston Branch) was closed following Lambley colliery's closure.

CHAPTER 9

From the Great War
to Nationalisation

The Last Pre-grouping Years

World War I saw the internal combustion engine prove its worth, and after initial post-war depression, the motor vehicle, car, lorry and bus, was to come into its own to the disadvantage of the railways. On the N & CR system, there were no major changes up to 1923. In common with all our railways the NER and NBR rolling stock was far from showing signs of excellent maintenance or general appearance, and with change in the air, the North British company in particular showed reluctance to invest in improvements when its own existence was limited.

On the N & CR main line, the McDonnell 4–4–0s of Class 38 were having their swan song, and early Worsdell 4–4–0s were shortly to largely monopolise passenger workings between Newcastle and Carlisle. The BTP tanks were also disappearing, leaving later tank classes to dominate Newcastle–Hexham services. The usual wide range of tender classes could be found on goods and mineral workings, including some of the new T2 0–8–0s designed by Raven. Of the 1919–20 locomotives, Nos 2254, 2257–8 went to Carlisle shed, and Nos 2260–2, 2266–7, 2269 were at Blaydon in 1920 and a host were at Gateshead sheds.

As a wartime economy, the NER suspended the passenger service on the Brampton Town branch from 1 March 1917, and resumption came on 1 March 1920. Traffic was light, however, and it was to be finally withdrawn three years later, and the branch closed (so much for the 50 years).

165

LNER—A Unified "Carlisle System"

The formation of the London & North Eastern Railway in 1923 unified the NER and NBR, so at last the Border Counties section became part of the same concern as the other lines. In fact, the LNER wisely did little to disrupt long-established practice, and the BCR retained its Scottish flavour and individuality up to nationalisation, indeed up to its closure. North British rolling stock remained the rule on this line, which was in the company's South Scottish area. At Carlisle, the NB Waverley Route gave the LNER two "main" entries to Carlisle and this allowed greater movement of rolling stock between the ex-NB ("Canal") and NER depots. In particular, former NB locomotives occasionally headed N & CR trains and the London Road depot would contain NB locomotives at times. The Midland Railway had become part of the LMSR, and thus locomotives sporting *LMS* traversed the western extremity of the N & CR.

Sadly, the period from 1923 to 1948 could not be regarded as one of growth in any respect on the N & CR system, rather one of, at best, stagnation, at worst, slow decay. In any case money was limited for improvements. The motor age was growing up, and sapping railway traffic. Many bus operators sprang up working between Newcastle and Hexham in particular, but also competing for the Newcastle–Carlisle trade. Even Newcastle Corporation was a major competitor, with its trams to Lemington and Newburn, and buses to Ryton, Prudhoe and Branch End (Stocksfield). The private car was a minor menace as yet, but motor lorries took much short-haul goods, especially agricultural traffic. Fortunately, the really bulky mineral traffic, except for very short haulage, remained with the railways.

Motive Power Survey

In the early 1920s, the important depot at Blaydon had locomotives of a dozen classes for passenger, goods and mineral work, the most numerous types being the Class E 0–6–0T for shunting,

Class C 0–6–0, Class P–P3 0–6–0, T2/T3 0–8–0, and O 0–4–4T. From the pre-Worsdell era remained one 398 0–6–0, and a 59 0–6–0. Carlisle had some 2–4–0s and 4–4–0s for the passenger trips. A few NB locomotives used on the BCR were reallocated to Blaydon, such as 4–4–0T No 1401 (ex-No 72) built in 1880 by Drummond (withdrawn in 1924), 4–4–0 tender locomotives and 4–4–2Ts (particularly the Reid Class M, also known as "Yorkies") were common on BCR duties, with the ubiquitous 0–6–0 tender classes. The LNER gradually replaced the very old-fashioned non–corridor NB carriages with more modern stock.

In the later 1920s and 1930s, the Q Class 4–4–0s of the NER became one of the most familiar types on passenger trains along the main line, while the various passenger tank classes monopolised the Hexham–Newcastle locals. In the mid-1930s Gresley's D49 4–4–0 type reached the line; both "Shire" and "Hunt" types were allocated. The Class R 4–4–0s also appeared frequently. New Gresley V1 2–6–2Ts appeared in the mid-1930s. Reid 4–4–0s became common on the BCR trains. Many other types from ex-NER and ex-NB origin could appear on the line however, especially from the Gateshead sheds. Even LNER main line 4–4–2s and 4–6–2s could make an appearance, being used on the east coast route, while eventually LNER Pacifics were used on the Waverley Route also.

By the later 1930s, apart from new locomotives, the sense of "stagnation" must have been rather obvious on the N & CR, as so very little change had occurred in any significant way to the way and works, unlike NER days, when things always seemed to be being altered. On the bus competition front, the whole Newcastle–Carlisle section was the preserve largely of United Automobile Services of Darlington in which the LNER had a part interest. The United Carlisle–Newcastle service No 34 remains to this day (becoming 334 and joint with Ribble). United had also taken over the Newcastle Corporation "south bank of the Tyne" services.

Double Demise

Two branches proved too uneconomic to retain existing services. The Brampton Town line passenger services ceased on 29 October 1923, goods traffic was ended on 31 December, and the tracks taken up in 1924—a quick end to a section of line with an interesting history. The rest of the Brampton Railway remained in use.

The Hexham & Allendale line was next for pruning. Inevitably, motor buses were plying from Hexham into Allendale Town via Langley and Haydon Bridge and the Allendale station was, to say the least, not well-sited. The passenger service ended on 22 September 1930, but in this case, goods traffic continued. In 1924 the line had three passenger trains each way plus one extra each way on Tuesdays, and remarkable to relate, a Sunday train each way (4.10pm from Hexham; 5.05pm from Allendale). More remarkable, the 4.10pm from Hexham was in fact a through train from Newcastle Central, and the 5.05pm train was similar. Following closure, the LNER timetable in 1931 stated: "A frequent bus service is operated by Emerson's services between Hexham station and Allendale and Allenheads, giving connections with trains from Newcastle and Carlisle, and serving Haydon Bridge, Langley, Staward, Catton, Lowgate, Sinderhope and Sparty Lea en route. For particulars, apply at local stations." Some years later, United acquired Emersons services, and initiated routes 37–38 from Newcastle to Allenheads, via Hexham.

Timetable Survey—Carlisle, Alston, North Wylam

Throughout the inter-war period, the LNER continued to enjoy the wealth of coal traffic in the Tyneside area, offsetting the decline in passenger traffic through road competition. Worst affected by this was the urban fringe of Newcastle, especially Scotswood, Lemington, Newburn, Blaydon and Ryton. The Carlisle–Newcastle service, so much quicker than a bus, was less af-

168

fected. The Alston branch had an advantage over the local road system, one which was to serve well in prolonging its life, in that there was no good road of A or B standard from Alston to Haltwhistle, as the Alston–Brampton road diverged westwards over Tindale Fells from near Lambley, leaving a series of narrow winding lanes in the Featherstone area. A very steep hill by the South Tyne at Coanwood was another handicap to any bus operator. But having said this, it must be recalled that the already thin population density of the Alston region was still declining. The train service was no money-spinner.

The N & CR line service in mid-1924 can be outlined as follows. The down trains on weekdays were at 12.40am (the "Paddy"—through carriage to Stranraer), 5.45am (Hexham), 6.10am (Hawick), 6.37am (Carlisle), 7.35am (Hexham), 8.15am (Carlisle), 8.50am (Hexham), 9.45am (Hexham), 10.17am SO (Carlisle), 10.30am (Carlisle), 10.50am (Hawick), 11.00am SO (Hexham), 11.45am (Hexham), 12.20pm SO (Hexham), 12.40pm (Hexham), 1.18pm (Carlisle, but SO Silloth), 1.25pm SO (Hexham) SX (Wylam), 1.45pm (Hexham), 2.15pm (Carlisle), 2.40pm SO (Carlisle), 2.55pm (Carlisle), 3.45pm (Hexham), 4.27pm (Hawick), 4.50pm (Hexham), 5.20pm (Carlisle), 5.25pm SX (Hexham), 5.50pm (Hexham), 6.20pm (Carlisle), 6.25pm SX (Wylam), 6.50pm (Hexham), 7.50pm (Hexham), 8.40pm (Carlisle), 8.55pm (Hexham), 9.50pm (Hexham, but SO Haltwhistle), 11.08pm ThSO (Hexham). The up service was similar. The down Sunday trains left Newcastle at 7.25am (Carlisle), 10.05am (Hexham), 2.40pm (Allendale), 5.30pm (Hexham), 6.20pm (Carlisle), 8.55pm (Hexham) giving a similar up service. The two Newcastle–Carlisle Sunday trains are noteworthy for their long-standing existence. To complete the picture on week-days there were two Brampton Junction–Carlisle trains each way; down at 2.10pm and 5.45pm from Brampton Junction.

The Alston Branch service at this time comprised four trains each way on weekdays, one down train being at a different time on Saturdays from M–F.

The North Wylam branch, suffering from the tram competition east from Newburn, and with its other two stations both at disadvantages, Heddon being over a mile south of the village it served, allowing buses easy advantage and North Wylam having Wylam station so close, had a service which was by-and-large reduced over the inter-war period. There were occasional promotional attempts by the LNER but with limited chance of success. Thus a Sunday service was revived on 7 March 1931 with nine trains each way, none stopping at Heddon. At the same period, the basic weekday service was of 19 down trains (plus a few extras), and 16 up trains. By 1947 the down weekday service had 14 trains (plus one SO), and 16 up trains (plus one SO). The Sunday service was of five trains each way, with no stop at Heddon. Throughout its existence, very little use of the branch had been made for through passenger services west of Wylam, but in 1947 one stopping train, the 9.45am ex-Newcastle on weekdays, ran to Haltwhistle. For through goods from Carlisle for Newcastle, the line did provide a means of by-passing possible congestion at Blaydon. For some reason the LNER renamed Prudhoe station Ovingham in 1935, a title retained till 1938, when it became (and remains) Prudhoe for Ovingham. Ovingham, a village over the Tyne, was a much smaller place.

The 1947 service on the N & CR main line had the usual comprehensive look. The first down train was the by now usual "boat train", the express to Carlisle for the benefit of Stranraer passengers, and this ran via North Wylam. For many years afterwards, indeed up to the closure of the branch, the "Paddy" ran non-stop via North Wylam, in some years with a request stop (by prior arrangement) at Hexham. I recall several of these post-midnight journeys to Carlisle in 1966 and rattling in a diesel unit over Wylam bridge, on the first stage to Belfast. The first "regular" down departure was the 5.50am to Riccarton Junction and the last train was the 11.05pm for Hexham. The Sunday service was basically of ten down trains (five to Carlisle, five to Hexham), and eleven up trains, which included the "Saturday night Paddy", 2.30am express from Carlisle.

For the Alston line, with its usual G5 haulage, there were seven down trains plus, for the revellers, a 10.10pm SO. Up trains were also seven, and a SO departure at 9.05pm. No Sunday service was operated.

By 1947, with traffic at certain stations on the main line often very low, the timetable had began to show trains not stopping at certain stations, a trend which was to increase. On the N & CR main line, the stations most affected were Scotby, Naworth, Ryton, Scotswood and Elswick. All, save Naworth, had strong bus competition. Naworth was simply remote from likely passengers. On the Alston branch, no intermediate station was unimportant in this sense; every passenger helped. Non-stopping was never to be countenanced.

North Tynedale Notes

Under LNER auspices, the long-fostered NB notion of the Border Counties being a main line to Scotland was discarded. The BCR and the Wansbeck Valley line were rural by-ways. The BCR was in addition the shortest route between Newcastle and the border woollen town of Hawick, with 25,000 or so souls.

But, as with so many now-vanished rural British railways, the BCR was part of the countryside it served, a link with the outside world, a friendly, familiar and indeed necessary part of life. At stations such as Chollerton and Tarset, the post office was in the station buildings. For many years, one of the most interesting trains on the line was a nightly Edinburgh–Newcastle beer train. In about 1923 on a frosty night, the train became derailed at Acomb colliery junction, near Wall, and the barrels burst, the beer froth freezing. Men clearing the line after sunrise filled their "bait cans" with the "melting" beer. At the same period, one Billy Niven often drove the beer train, and as it passed through Bellingham in the small hours, would toot his whistle several times for the benefit of his sweetheart in the town. Each September there was a great burst of activity for a day, with the

171

annual Bellingham show (officially, the North Tyne and Redesdale Agricultural Show) attracting many people from Hexham and Tyneside. Apparently there was also cause for extra trains occasionally, with the Bellingham–Plashetts football matches.

The line was never easy to operate, with its long single-line stretches, a ruling gradient of 1 in 100, limited passing loops, occasional severe curves, and weight restrictions. Only at Reedsmouth could two normal-length passenger trains pass one another, and thus timetabling had to allow for a meeting of down and up passenger services at Reedsmouth. Yet the line was part of the social structure of North Tynedale and when closure came it had many bitter mourners. In the non-corridor NB coaches, farmers would chat and smoke their pipes, often with a bag of potatoes, crate of poultry or even a pig, in the compartment beside them. One day it is related a playful chap put his girlfriend's ball of knitting wool outside the carriage window trapped in the frame to hide it from her. Unfortunately it unravelled, and the wool ran for miles up the line north of Hexham before unravelling, and next day a ganger walked the track and wound it all up for her unwinding it from bushes, brambles, hawthorns, fields and even trees. For villagers and isolated farmsteads, mail, parcels and milk cans were awaited or delivered at the station. The Border Counties was a gem of a railway.

In the inter-war period, the most important change in the region was the afforestation of the Kielder area, the Forestry Commission (set up in 1918) planting thousands of conifers in particular over the hillsides and valley slopes and Kielder Forest, as it has become, is one of the biggest in England. (An incidental point; the LNER removed the anomalous NB spelling of "Keilder", to its correct form, for the station.) In Autumn 1933 a new Lewiefield Halt was opened $1\frac{1}{2}$ miles north of Plashetts, with wooden platform and waiting rooms, appropriate as it served new forestry housing. The forestry developments in the area helped to ease the burden of the run-down of the Plashetts coal mines which were becoming uneconomic; some miners became forest workers. The other mine served by a short branch,

Acomb colliery, was to last longer being closer to markets, although lorries were to abstract traffic from the line. Two stations were re-named in the period. In August 1919 the NBR changed Chollerford to Humshaugh after the village one mile to the north, to avoid the confusion of the name with Chollerton; 1948 saw Kielder renamed as Kielder Forest. In World War II, the bleak hillside station of Saughtree was closed as an economy measure on 1 December 1944 (to reopen on 23 August 1948). One wonders what its patrons did in the period of closure—walk the road to Deadwater, a goodly tramp, or if fit, stagger over the hilltop to Riccarton, or safer, walk the line itself to the junction. Wall station suffered severe fire damage in the war period, and wooden buildings were erected to replace those burnt down. Before the war the stationmaster at Deadwater (the north end of whose platform was in Scotland) was Miss Margaret Wylie who, in addition to her office and platform chores, operated the two-lever ground frame for the up and down signals. On this exposed northern end of the line severe wintry weather could necessitate a snow plough coming out from Riccarton.

Regarding traffic generally, apart from coal, stone from quarries in the Chollerton–Humshaugh area was significant, the main quarries being Barrasford, Swinburn, Brunton, Fallowfield and Black Pasture. Livestock traffic, particularly cattle and milk, was also reasonable, and the Newcastle, Hexham, Bellingham, Morpeth and Hawick markets were local venues; at Scots Gap there was a weekly cattle auction mart, and this was significantly located near the railway station at that place on the Wansbeck line. Sheep, being reared throughout the Northumbrian Fells region, were also important.

The pleasant old market town (or large village) of Bellingham was the biggest settlement on the line, (with the parish of Bellingham having 1287 people in 1931), and there was a fair amount of passengers down to Hexham, with its bigger market and greater retailing facilities. Presumably to avoid any possible confusion with the London suburb, the station was officially made "Bellingham (North Tyne)" about 1947. The link towards

173

Morpeth and Reedsmouth, via the Wansbeck Valley line, required reversal there by the occasional timetabled through trains, but operating convenience meant that more often there was a change of trains at Reedsmouth. However, the turntable at Reedsmouth was vital for any locomotives moving between the lines. The sidings here were useful for the various goods movements.

At the very end of the LNER regime in October 1947, the timetable of passenger trains on the BCR was as follows. Three trains from Central station departed from Hexham at 6.51am, 12.07pm and 5.10pm, the first being for Riccarton, the other two for Hawick. The up trains were similar, leaving Riccarton Junction at 6.47am, 10.30am, and 5.03pm, the middle train being from Riccarton, the other two ex-Hawick. A note stated that the 6.47am up train called at Deadwater at 6.55am when taking-on passengers who had informed the Riccarton Junction stationmaster of their intention before 5.00pm on the day prior to their journey. The station at Thorneyburn, long subject to trains stopping only on Tuesdays, was by now seeing only one down train on Saturdays, and two up trains on Saturdays (one to take up only), or Wednesday and Saturday only to set down only. In addition, Bellingham had a daily 4.05pm extra to Scots Gap via Reedsmouth, and an arrival from the Wansbeck at 3.09pm. As ever, no Sunday service ran. By 1948 the most common passenger locomotives were the Reid Scott class 4–4–0s, but ex-NB and NER 0–6–0s were not unusual. Some of the Scotts, such as Nos 2435 *Norna*, 2425 *Ellangowan* and 2440 *Wandering Willie* (1946 numbers), were very familiar performers.

"Railcars"

In the early 1920s, the NER "steam autocars" began to disappear as the rather aged rebuilt BTPs were past their prime. Soon the LNER was seeking another way to reduce costs on branch services by using another method apart from a tank locomotive and one or two carriages. Sentinel steam railcars were purchased

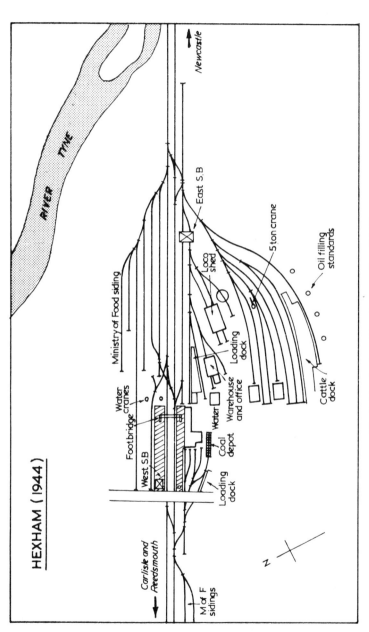

HEXHAM (1944)

RIVER TYNE

Newcastle

Carlisle and Reedsmouth

M of F sidings

West S.B

Loading dock

Footbridge

Water cranes

Coal depot

Water

Warehouse and office

Loading dock

Ministry of Food siding

East S.B

Loco shed

5 ton crane

Cattle dock

Oil filling standards

N

Fig 7 Track plan of Hexham station (1944)

and outlasted others bought from the Clayton company, and three Armstrong Whitworth diesel-electric railcars. However, use of Sentinels and Claytons on the Carlisle line was limited. An interesting minute in the records of the mechanical engineer, NE Area, for 1 November 1935 reads: "Indicator blind sent to the Equipment and Engineering Coy, 2–3 Norfolk Street, Strand, WC2, for lettering with 23 names, including Newcastle, Durham, Consett, Blackhill, Rowlands Gill, Lintz Green, Hexham, Blaydon, North Wylam, Bedlington etc."

In December 1946 the LNER was considering introducing ten AEC 210hp diesel-mechanical railcars on routes of gradient 1 in 66 or steeper, such as near Newcastle (eg Consett branch). In March 1947 the intention was for eleven for Newcastle, but nationalisation put paid to this. In any case, the cars would not have been for the Hexham or North Wylam services.

Locomotive Sheds

Hexham shed was destroyed by a fire in about 1920, but was rebuilt. It was slightly damaged by an incendiary bomb in World War II. Locomotives allocated there in 1947 were five G5 0–4–4Ts and an ex-NBR 0–6–0 of Class J36. Blaydon shed had almost 80 locomotives officially stationed there in the late 1920s, 70 in 1941, and 84 in 1947. Alston had usually two, and Carlisle almost 40. The LNER transferred London Road shed to the South Scottish area in 1924 making it subsidiary to the NBR Canal shed. In 1933 it was closed. Its last allocation was 4 D17 2 4–4–0 (NE Q), 1 J21 0–6–0 (NE C), 1 J24 0–6–0 (NE P), 1 N8 0–6–2T (NE B), 1 Q6 0–8–0 (NE T2), 2 D29 4–4–0 (NBR J), 1 D30 4–4–0 (NBR J) plus the *North Briton* Sentinel car. The Alston locomotives in early 1947 consisted of G5 0–4–4T (NE O) No 7315 and 0–6–0 No 5100. In Summer 1937 a rebuilt A8 4–6–2T No. 2146 was photographed on the branch service (see *LNER Album Vol 2* by B. Stephenson). The ex-NBR shed at Reedsmouth had NB 0–6–0s (Class J36) Nos 5331, 5343, and J21 0–6–0 No 5101. Two Class D32 4–4–0s, Nos 2448–9 (ex-

NBR Nos. 887–8) were at Blaydon in the twilight of their life. Several new V1 2–6–2Ts arrived at Blaydon before the war, eg No 465 in May 1936, later No 7659.

Carlisle Canal Shed had by 1947 five Gresley Pacifics for Waverley route trains, but on occasion one might stray onto the Newcastle service, as happened on one occasion in 1948, when A3 No 95 *Flamingo* was photographed on a four-coach train to Newcastle, passing Ryton. The Carlisle A3s were among the least-photographed Gresley locomotives. Among Canal's other types were D49 4–4–0s, K3 2–6–0s, J39 0–6–0s, J36 0–6–0s, G5 0–4–4Ts, and a pair of Holmes D31 4–4–0s, Nos 2059, 2065.

Messrs Vickers Armstrong Ltd, Scotswood works, contracted to repair many LNER locomotives in 1946–7, and in October 1947, for example, many Class O7 2–8–0s were being outshopped and temporarily based at Blaydon for trial runs before returning to their bases, such as Colwick. The works had its sidings and junction with the Carlisle line just east of Scotswood station. Vickers Armstrong had built in an earlier period some of the splendid NER T2s (Q6s), in particular.

177

CHAPTER 10

The N & CR since 1948

Economic Reality

Like all British railways, the Carlisle system of lines went into the 1950s facing harsh economic realities. Traffic overall was in decline, and the roads were resounding to an increasing density of cars, lorries and buses. Inevitably there were. . . .

Early Economies

In the first few years of British Railways (North Eastern Region), things carried on much as before, but an early event was the closure of the Allendale branch. The relatively small volume of goods traffic from the line did not warrant the operating costs, and the line was closed on 17 November 1950, 20 years after the ending of passenger trains. Usually an 0–6–0 locomotive from Hexham worked the branch goods.

On the main line, the very rural Naworth station was closed on 5 May 1952, and in the same year Elswick station was closed on Sundays to passenger trains. Ryton succumbed on 5 July 1954 after an unequal battle against more convenient bus services. The section of line from Newcastle to Scotswood Bridge junction lost one passenger service on 1 February 1954, when the service to Blackhill was withdrawn. Goods traffic ceased at Wetheral from 1 April 1955, while on the Alston branch the intermediate stations were reduced to unstaffed halts in the same period. Coanwood lost its goods traffic at the same time, 19 September 1955. Not far distant, almost without being noticed except by the locals, the historic Brampton Railway was closed in

Wall station was axed completely on 15 September 1958, Lemington and Newburn closing to passengers at the same time. Goods continued at the latter two until 4 January 1960, but a coal depot at Lemington remained open till 6 July 1964. In Cumberland, How Mill was completely closed on 5 January 1959, and Low Row closed to passengers only at the same date. The goods facilities at Low Row were converted to a private delivery siding and remained till 1965. Scotby station, virtually in an outlying suburb of Carlisle, was closed completely on 2 November 1959. Corbridge lost its gantry signalbox in this period, when sparks from a steam locomotive set fire to birds' nests and the wood burst into flames. On the Alston branch goods services ended at Lambley and Slaggyford on 12 September 1960. The former station, at the south end of Lambley viaduct, and once so busy with coal and lime off the Lambley Fell branch, became a sleepy halt like the others on the line. The great days were very much in the past. Alston station was still fairly busy however; in 1952 goods traffic was 11,858 tons (receipts £15,855).

The coming of diesel multiple-units allowed the closure of Hexham depot on 6 April 1959, and the small Alston shed on 27 September 1959. Blaydon shed retained many goods locomotives, but soon lost its passenger locomotives as a result of the dieselisation. It lost its steam allocation in 1963 being closed and demolished within two years, apart from a fairly newly-built mess building, which was left empty and quickly vandalised.

Allocations of steam locomotives in October 1954 included 2–6–0s Nos 43128 and 76024 at Alston, 0–4–4Ts 67249, 67265/70, 67309/16/29 and 0–6–0 65119 at Hexham, and eight J39 0–6–0s, 17 Q6 0–8–0s, 13 K1 2–6–0s, eight G5s and six V1/V3 2–6–2Ts amongst Blaydon's allocation. The dieselisation of this and other North Eastern areas spelt the scrap heap for the old Worsdell 0–4–4Ts in a very short space of time. Alston's last locomotive was No 77011, which it may be recalled headed one of the final Border Counties trains. In the 1950s, another locomotive class common on both passenger and goods services on the N & CR was the Thompson B1 Class 4–6–0, and Gateshead shed had a number of these including some of the named examples. As late as Autumn 1966, a B1 was seen on a goods train passing through Blaydon, when in the twilight of steam operations, K1, Q6, WD and J27 locomotives were most common locally.

At the beginning of 1960 new English Electric Type 4 (Class 40) locomotives were allocated to Gateshead for operating selected passenger, goods and parcel, trains on the Newcastle–Edinburgh, Newcastle–York/Leeds routes, and on the N & CR line for staff experience of the type (not planned to operate on this line for regular purposes). These were just the first of many main-line diesel classes which regularly appeared on the N & CR, mainly on goods workings, by the late 1960s.

Showing the North Eastern Region not to be lacking in promotional drive, in mid-1958 a day-touring ticket named the "Day-line Diesel" ticket was introduced, primarily for use on the new diesel trains, but valid on steam and electric services. The "Northern Section" ticket covered NER lines from Alnwick to Whitby Town, including the N & CR. The ticket cost 75p (half price for under 14s), and with it the purchaser received a souvenir brooch bearing a silver-coloured relief of a diesel coach surrounded by an enamelled circle in North Eastern orange and the words "British Railways NE Region".

On Through the Sixties

The new chairman of BR, Dr Beeching, soon cast an appraising eye on the north-east railway system. One of his reports envisaged closure of the Newcastle–Berwick line, channelling all traffic from Newcastle to the west coast route at Carlisle. On the N & CR only a Newcastle–Carlisle service would be left, the locals and local stations would all go. The line had lately increased in importance following the closure of the Stainmore railway from Darlington across the Pennines in 1962. The Tyneside–Blackpool summer passenger trains had taken this route, and were switched to the N & CR. There was also a steady mineral traffic diverted to the N & CR, including Cumbrian limestone (and other stone) to the Tees steelworks, and chemical works, and coal/coke from south-west Durham to Cumberland.

Beeching economies on the N & CR were not long delayed. During 1963 the Consett branch was finally closed completely, lessening the importance of Blaydon as a railway centre. In 1965 no less than 14 stations lost their goods facilities in pursuit of the policy of eliminating local wagon-load traffic. Those closed were Scotswood, Wylam, Prudhoe, Stocksfield, Riding Mill, Corbridge, Fourstones, Haydon Bridge, Bardon Mill, Greenhead, Gilsland, Low Row (PDS), Brampton Junction and Alston. (Featherstone Park had officially lost goods facilities on 9 December 1963.) The Alston branch operations could now be simplified, and all signalling was removed, except for a few forlorn NER distants which remained like stark sentinels till closure of the line. Unmanned and ungated level-crossings were set up, road users having to exercise caution and commonsense.

Early in the 1960s the NE Region had opened the large Tyne marshalling yard at Lamesley, south of Low Fell, to serve the Newcastle area, rendering most local goods yards redundant. Thus Blaydon's many sidings were reduced, leaving, when the locomotive shed closed in 1965, only two running lines from Scotswood Bridge to Blaydon station junction. Just to the east of the junction a small goods and coal depot was left operational with a few sidings by the Redheugh branch. This line had increased in importance with the opening of Tyne yard; Tyne–Carlisle goods now all traversed the Gateshead–Dunston–Blaydon line. Coal from east Durham to Stella power station, and returning empties, also took the line. In 1966 the link from Scotswood Bridge to the Redheugh line facing east (Blaydon Main junction) was closed and removed.

The early 1960s unfortunately were also seeing mining contract in the Blaydon–Prudhoe district, with the mines closing through exhaustion or their being uneconomic. West Wylam colliery was one of the most famous to close. A bright point marginally, was the opening of a large paper mill (Kimberley–Clark) at Prudhoe, but much use of road transport was made. The creamery at Stocksfield (opened about 1936), with a siding from the N & CR, also was using road transport by now.

1966 was the twilight year of local BR steam. English Electric Class 37 diesel-electrics based at Gateshead were common on goods and mineral trains, with the occasional Class 24, 40, and 47. Later Clayton Class 17 diesels appeared and, briefly, EE Class 20s, with small Class 03 and 04 shunters on shunting work, for example at Blaydon. From the Carlisle end, Class 40 and 47 diesel-electrics were usual on the N & CR goods. Until 1967 a few surviving steam locomotives were rostered to the Stella (and North Stella) coal trains, usually Class Q6 0–8–0, J27 0–6–0, WD 2–8–0, and K1 2–6–0. On a few odd occasions, a Carlisle Kingmoor Britannia is believed to have traversed the N & CR, but this is not documented. By 1968 it was all diesels.

In 1965–6 the construction of a new road bridge over the Tyne at Scotswood to replace the old 1820s chain bridge had effect on the railway. Approach road construction in Scotswood meant the virtual demolition of the old "village" and alterations to the embankment of the railway and a new rail bridge over the Newburn road. To do this, the line from Blaydon to Scotswood junction was closed at various times, on Sundays, and later for several weeks whilst the works were undertaken. In these periods, all traffic used the North Wylam route, and buses were hired from United Automobile Services, to run between Blaydon and Scotswood stations for Blaydon passengers.

The dawn of 1967 was another bad time for the line. BR had asked the Ministry of Transport to be allowed to close to passengers many of the remaining N & CR stations. On 2 January 1967, the stations at Elswick, Fourstones, Gilsland, Greenhead, Heads Nook and Wetheral were closed. Particularly sad was the closing of Gilsland as rebuilt by NER, with its rather attractive architecture, its well-kept garden plots, and also its long association with the line for specials for the spa. In a few years, all had been virtually demolished, although in several cases the station houses remained in private use. Scotswood was also due to close, when the constructional activities there had concluded, and it ceased operation on 1 May 1967. Blaydon was reprieved by the Minister, The Rt Hon Mrs Barbara Castle, MP, as it was felt a large urban area such as this should have a station, if the N & CR line was to have a service for bigger local communities. Eleven years later BR modernised the station; the old buildings were demolished and replaced by "bus-stop" type waiting shelters.

At the same time "paytrains" became the rule on the line, the Alston Branch and, until closure, the North Wylam line. Conductor-guards collected fares and issued tickets. All local booking offices etc were closed; only at Hexham was it possible to buy tickets for through journeys beyond the line, and later this disappeared although at Hexham, staff still remained for enquiries, and other duties. However, it all reduced costs. Finally for 1967, the North Eastern Region itself disappeared; it was merged into the Eastern Region, but York became the ER headquarters.

North Wylam Closure

The old Scotswood, Newburn & Wylam Railway was really a duplicate route between Scotswood and West Wylam. By the 1967 period, it had only one station open and this, North Wylam, was less than $\frac{1}{2}$-mile from Wylam station. As around Ryton, the collieries in the Newburn area had been or were closing down, leaving the North Stella power station as the only real generator of traffic. Despite the burst of activity in 1966–7 mentioned earlier and the nightly passage of the express Newcastle–Carlisle and reverse Irish trains, the line was really largely unnecessary. On 11 March 1968 the line was closed to all passenger traffic, and for goods from Newburn (North Stella) to West Wylam junction. The traffic was concentrated on the old N & CR. Gradually the line was singled from Scotswood junction through the tunnel and Lemington, and signalling was removed to leave it a long siding operated from Scotswood signalbox. The large redbrick Newburn and West Wylam signal boxes were demolished. George Stephenson's birthplace, east of Wylam, now looked out to a derelict railway, which was rather a pity. Also, the handsome West Wylam bridge was now open to vandalism, and possible demolition.

In 1972 the *Evening Chronicle* for 1 April published the news of a "Walk Plan for Line". It stated:

> The disused railway line between Newburn and Wylam may have a new life ahead—as a scenic public walkaway. The proposal, presented in a report to Northumberland Planning Committee will be one of the topics in discussions between members of Hexham and Newburn councils over the future of the line. British Rail are being asked to allow time for the talks before disposing of the line, and to name their price for it and the West Wylam railway bridge. The councils will be asked for their views on future uses of the line and on the proposal to use it as part of a riverside park project.

[The 1969 Tyne Recreational Study recommended a country park beside the Tyne between Newburn and Wylam]

> The study also recommends that an extensive footpath system should be provided within the park, and the report to the committee suggests that the line could be used as a pleasant walkway. This would provide an effective link with Stephenson's cottage and Wylam station yard could also be reclaimed and landscaped. It is also suggested that West Wylam Bridge, built in 1876, and of some historical value, could be preserved to form a useful link in the footpath system.

Alston Branch—A Respite

Inevitably, the Beeching proposals had no place for lines such as the Alston branch. It had to go. BR's attempts in 1963 came to nought, when Mr Ernest Marples, MP, the then Minister of Transport, upheld objections by local councils and MPs (and also lesser mortals) and prevented closure. Most of the objections related to the inadequate road system, problem of transport for school children to Haltwhistle, and the winter weather of South Tynedale, and Alston frequently becoming cut off by road. On Easter Sunday 1967, many rail enthusiasts visited the branch when Class 4 2–6–0 No 43121 headed the Stephenson Locomotive Society's special train, the "Scottish Rambler". In 1967 the branch timetable showed seven down trains and one SO extra, and six up trains plus two extras SO. No Sunday service, as ever.

A second closure attempt came at the start of the seventies. *The Daily Telegraph* for 16 October 1970 reported: "Renewed attempt to close rail 'lifeline'." It stated that

last year . . . the Minister of Transport did not propose to continue the £43,000 a year subsidy for the line after 1970. As a result, British Railways has now given formal notice to close the line. An alternative bus service has been proposed but this is being opposed because it would mean that the isolated villages of Lambley and Coanwood, which are without a major road, would be without transport of any sort. At present they are served by the railway line. A conference has been called by the Haltwhistle and Alston councils with all parish councils concerned, so as to collate objections which will be put to the North East and North West Transport Users' Consultative Councils. This week the two councils were surprised to learn that Northumberland County Council was surveying and prospecting for a new road from Featherstone to Lambley which would not be impossible in winter as is the present route. Often in winter the railway is the lifeline for Alston, the highest market town in England—and the main objection to the line's closure is likely to be that it is socially necessary for the two rural areas. British Rail consider the line is uneconomic and that too few people travel on it, but if it closes there is the need to maintain 44 bridges including Lambley viaduct, one of the finest pieces of Victorian railway architecture in the country.

Indeed, the Northumberland council was planning a new road, to by-pass the Lambley–Coanwood hills and narrow sharp bends. Thus it was no surprise when building of the road began, for the formal notice of closure of the line to be announced in January 1973, to take place when the new road and alternative bus services were available. Licences for the latter were eventually awarded to Ribble, part of the National Bus Company. BR had stated that the cost of running the line in 1972 was £77,000 a year. The Alston branch finally closed on 1 May 1976, Ribble service 681 replacing the trains and traversing the new section of road near Lambley and Coanwood.

187

Preservation?

The long notice of closure helped to foster the interest of preservationists for the railway, and the South Tynedale Preservation Society emerged in April 1973 with the ambitious aim of preserving the entire branch, or failing that, part of it at the Alston end, running both a service on the line and a tourist attraction using steam locomotives bought for the purpose. Even in 1975 the society had acquired a small tank engine, which was stored at Slaggyford. However, railway preservation is expensive. In March 1975 the figure of £250,000 was given as the cost of buying the line. Mr John Parker, a Haltwhistle plumbing contractor, was chairman of the society, and he stated: "We will have to have a public company to buy the line. It will be a lengthy business with a lot of legal procedure. We reckon there will be about a year's gap between British Rail leaving and us taking the line over." He added that a New York well-wisher had already sent £5. But the STRPS has shown determination, and has good support, and has adopted methods of raising finance such as organising rail tours, selling Christmas cards, and raising capital by offering shares. Inflation in 1976–7 damaged its efforts, and in December 1976 it was reported that the railway authorities had assured the society that the 1½ miles of track at the Alston end would be left in site until 17 February, provided that STRPS raised £40,800 as the cost of this stretch and the station. However, the huge and escalating cost of the scheme has meant that the STRPS has had to modify its aims which now consist of buying Alston station and a mile or so of track bed on which to lay a narrow gauge railway.

Bellingham Finale

In the North Tyne valley, the last short length of the Border Counties line closed with the withdrawal of goods services west of Woodburn (Wansbeck Valley Branch) on 11 November 1963. Usually, ex-NER 0–6–0s from Blyth worked the service before closure. Rails at Bellingham had lasted just over a century. Reedsmouth became a defunct railway village. It is fitting here to add that BR closed the Waverley Route on 6 January 1969, and Riccarton Junction became another such ghost village.

Traction in the 1970s

The diesel multiple-units (dmu) introduced in the late 1950s still operate most N & CR passenger trains. In the early 1970s there was a nice variation when one late evening train from Newcastle to Hexham was regularly worked by a Gateshead Class 24 or 25 with three or four carriages—Nos 5096, 7586, 7593, 7596 were seen on this working. Of the various classes on goods, the Clayton Class 17s, rather unpopular, went off to Scotland and early withdrawal, and Brush Class 31s arrived at Gateshead from further south on the ER. These often work in pairs on mineral trains. Occasionally a Class 50 worked a Carlisle–Tyne train before they all vanished in 1976 to the Western Region, to become the new Warship class. No 50 034 was seen at Tyne on 6 March 1976, having come in with a Carlisle goods.

For rail enthusiasts however, the occasional steam special with a preserved locomotive has been a highlight. Such tours were quite common before steam was banned in 1968; A4 No 60019 *Bittern*, for instance, headed a Waverley railtour from Leeds to Edinburgh on 12 November 1966, via Newcastle, North Wylam and Carlisle. In 1972 the N & CR was host to No 4498 *Sir Nigel Gresley*, which worked from Newcastle to Carlisle and back on a special on 17 June and attracted many people to watch it. Unfortunately BR did not continue to allow the line to be used for further specials, probably a tribute to its fairly busy traffic.

Upper Denton Incidents

The level-crossing on a by-road at Upper Denton, Cumberland, received some notoriety in 1970. BR had installed automatic crossings on many of its lines on minor road crossings, and sev-

eral were made on the N & CR. Blenkinsopp crossing near Greenhead was so treated, but because this was a main road (A69), the
adjoining signalbox was left, so that in normal hours a railway-
man could quickly meet any emergency by switching the signals
on the line to danger. At Upper Denton however, there was no
signalbox. Lt Col I.K.A. McNaughton reported on an accident
on 24 December 1970, when a private car skidded on the crossing which was frosty and slippery and became stuck on the cattle
grid, fouling both railway lines. While it was there the automatic
half barriers lowered and the car was struck by the 19.55 diesel
multiple-unit from Carlisle, which carried the vehicle 200yd
along the line. There were no passenger injuries, but the train
driver suffered considerable shock. When the car had been found
to be unmovable on the grid, an occupant of a following car
attempted to use the emergency telephones, but was unable to
find one. The Inspecting Officer was informed of six previous incidents at the crossing, in four of which the car drivers were
misled by the aspect of the crossing at night and made premature
turns to the left onto the railway line. Also, in four incidents, one
of which was the subject of an enquiry, the emergency telephones
had not been used. Recommendations were made in the report
for improving the visual impact of the crossing, where the road
crosses the tracks at a very acute angle, so that there would be a
distance of 118ft 6in between the barriers, and for providing a
non-skid surface. Local lighting to improve the visibility of the
emergency telephones was installed soon after the accident.
There are no nearby houses, and the darkness of a winter night
must have masked their location.

Kielder Water

In the mid-1970s the authority was given by the government for
the Northumbrian Water Authority to construct a £100 million
reservoir in North Tynedale at Kielder. In April 1977 with work
there under way, BR began a three-year contract to carry cement
from the Ribblesdale Cement Co at Clitheroe (Lancs) to

Hexham station, via Carlisle, in trains of 15 *Presflo* wagons. The cement would be discharged at Hexham into road lorries for the trip north. Some 10,000 tons of cement per year was involved. The new lake, Kielder Water, will no doubt become a scenic attraction in the border country in the 1980s.

Epitaph

As this is written in 1979, the N & CR seems a line with a secure future, and the only question is, when will modern rolling stock be given to the passengers? The multiple units are becoming aged and what will replace them? Is there ever a chance of "third rail" electrification between Newcastle and Hexham, especially with the Tyne & Wear Metro as an example of Newcastle's forward thinking? As ever, time will tell, and the N & CR has plenty of that. England's oldest cross-country (almost coast to coast) line still survives. Will it reach its 200th anniversary?

Appendices

APPENDIX 1
N & CR Locomotives taken over by NER 1862

NER No	N&CR No	Name	Builder	Date
453	4	*Hercules*	Hawthorn	1857
454	5	*Samson*	,,	1836
455	6	*Goliath*	,,	1836
456	7	*Atlas*	Robert Stephenson	1861
457	8	*Tyne*	Hawthorn	1861
458	9	*Eden*	Robert Stephenson	1861
459	10	*Lightning*	Thompson	1837
460	11	*Newcastle*	Hawthorn	1860
461★	12	*Carlisle*	,,	1860
462	13	*Wellington*	,,	1838
463	14	*Victoria*	Thompson	1838
464	15	*Nelson*	Hawthorn	1838
465†	16	*Northumberland*	,,	1838
466	17	*Cumberland*	,,	1838
467	18	*Durham*	,,	1839
468†	19	*Sun*	,,	1839
469	21	*Matt. Plummer*	Thompson	1839
470	22	*Adelaide*	,,	1840
471	23	*Mars*	,,	1840
472‡	24	*Jupiter*	,,	1840
473‡	25	*Venus*	,,	1841
474	26	*Saturn*	,,	1841
475	27	*Globe*	Hawthorn	1846
476★	28	*Planet*	,,	1846
477‡	29	*Albert*	,,	1847
478	30	*Swift*	,,	1847
479★	31	*Collingwood*	,,	1848
480	32	*Allen*	,,	1848
481†	33	*Alston*	Robert Stephenson	1850
482†	34	*Hexham*	,,	1850
483	35	*Prudhoe*	Hawthorn	1852

484	36	*Naworth*	,,	1853
485♮	37	*Blenkinsopp*	Robert Stephenson	1853
486	38	*Bywell*	,,	1853
487*	39	*Dilston*	Hawthorn	1855
488	40	*Langley*	,,	1855
489	41	*Thirlwall*	Robert Stephenson	1855
490	42	*Lanercost*	,,	1855
491	43	*Featherstonehaugh*	Hawthorn	1857

* Rebuilt as 0–6–0ST to work Redheugh Incline: 476, 479 (1873); 461 (1881); 487 (1883).
† Rebuilt as 2–4–0 at Gateshead: 468 (1863); 481 (1869); 465, 482 (1872).
‡ Rebuilt as 2–4–0; Nos 472, 473, 477 (dates unknown).
♮ Rebuilt as 0–6–0 at Gateshead 1871.

APPENDIX 2

Newcastle & Carlisle Railway Company Rule Book

Extracts from 'Rules & Regulations', dated 1853, a copy once belonging to John Parker, appointed Clerk at Carlisle, 14 April 1845. These are rules and regulations approved at the Board of Directors' meeting on 25 October 1852

1 General Regulations

1. Each person is to *devote himself* exclusively to the *Company's service*, attending during the regulated hours of the day, and residing wherever he may be required.

2. He is to *obey* promptly all *instructions* he may receive from persons placed in authority over him by the Directors, and *conform to all the Regulations* of the Company.

3. All Officers and *Servants* of the Company *hold* their *appointments* during the pleasure of the Directors, and the *following Regulation* has been made applicable thereto:-

Any Officer or Servant may be discharged from the Company's service (without caused assigned) on received the periods of notice enumerated below, or the equivalent wages—Clerks and Station Agents, one month; Guards, Enginemen, Firemen, Mechanics, Porters, Pointsmen & C., two weeks, or they will be liable to *immediate dismissal* for disobedience of orders, negligence, *misconduct*, or incompetency.

4. No instance of *intoxication* on duty will ever be overlooked, and

besides being *dismissed*, the offender will be liable to be punished by a magistrate.

5. Any person using improper language, or *cursing* and *swearing* while on duty will be liable to *dismissal*.

6. No person is allowed to receive any *gratuity* from the public on pain of *dismissal*.

7. Any instance of *rudeness* or incivility to passengers will meet with instant *punishment*.

8. Every person receiving *uniform* must appear in it when on duty *clean* and neat, and if any article provided by the Company shall be *improper used* or damaged, the party will be required *to make it good*.

9. *No person* is allowed, under any circumstances to *absent himself* from his duty *without permission*, from the Head Officer of his department. In case of unavoidable absence, through *sickness*, a *medical certificate* will be *required*.

10. No Servant is *to quit the Company's service* without giving *28 days* previous *notice*; *on leaving* the *service*, he must deliver up his uniform.

11. The Company reserve the right to deduct from the pay such sums as may be awarded for neglect of duty, such as *fines*, and for *rent*, when the servant is a tenant of the Company.

12. Should any *Servant* think himself *aggrieved* he may *memorialise* the Board; but in any such case the memorial must be sent *through* the *head* of his *department*.

13. *No Servant* is permitted to stand between waggons for the purpose of coupling them together while they are in motion; they must be coupled by reaching from the outside after having come together, and when at rest.

14. No Servant is permitted to *couple* and *uncouple* carriages or waggons while the Train is in motion.

2 Signals

RED is a signal of DANGER—STOP
GREEN is a signal of CAUTION—PROCEED SLOWLY
WHITE is a signal of ALL RIGHT—GO ON.

These signals will be made by circular discs or by FLAGS in the Day-time, and by *lamps* at Night. In addition to this, *any signal* or the arm, *waved* violently, denotes *danger*, and the necessity of stopping immediately. When the line is *clear* and nothing to impede the progress of the Train, *no signal* will be shown.

No *train* shall move on the main line *after Dark*, unless provided

195

with a Red Tail lamp, which is to be attached lighted to the last vehicle of the train.

At every Station there is a protecting Signal for each road, attached to fixed points, exhibiting a disc by day, and a lamp by night. From these points a *Red* Signal will be shown while a *Train* is stopping *at the Station*, and for *5 minutes* after its departure, when the *Green* Signal will be turned on for *5 minutes* more.

The Junctions and Termini are protected by signal posts; the *Red* signal is to be kept constantly shown at all these posts, and *no Engine* is allowed to *pass, until* in reply to the whistle, the signal has been turned off.

A *Red Board* or Flag, or an *extra Tail Lamp* by night, hung at the back of an Engine or Train *denotes* that an *Extra Train* is to follow.

3 *Fog*

Enginemen must make frequent use of the steam *whistle* during *Foggy Weather*. Also, when they are compelled to *stop on the road*, or from any other cause, are obliged to run at a *slower speed* than usual. During a *fog no engine* will be permitted to *start* from a Station if any Train has proceeded it within an interval of 10 minutes. Every *Driver* must therefore make it his duty *to ascertain* from the Station Clerk or Porter, "When the preceding train has started? and where is it next to Stop?"

No *Ballast Engine* shall run on the main line during *Fogs*.

4 *Regular*

Drivers must sound the steam whistle on approaching every station or level crossing, or when entering tunnels, or curves, where they cannot see $\frac{1}{2}$ mile before them. Two sharp whistles must be given "when danger is apprehended".

Every engine shall be *ready* and on the Departure line not less than 10 minutes before starting the Trains. The Engineman and Fireman both being in attendance at the same time.

Enginemen must *not* on any account, pass a station before the time specified in the TimeTable.

No Driver shall, when with a Train, *run* his Engine on the Main Line Tender first without the sanction of the Locomotive Superintendent.

Every *mineral train* must be shunted 15 minutes before a Passenger or Goods Train *is due*. If the passengers or goods train should be 10 minutes late, the mineral or goods train may proceed, provided the precautions required by the rules be attended to.

Two Passenger Trains shall not enter a station at the same time. Enginemen with Goods and Mineral trains are strictly prohibited from passing the Stations where Passenger Trains are stopping.

5 *Staff Rules (examples)*

Enginemen. *Smoking* is strictly prohibited within sight of the Stations, Platforms, or in the Engine sheds.

Guards. Every *Guard* is to be at the Station from which he is to start $\frac{1}{2}$ hour before the appointed time, that he may see to the marshalling of the carriages, and the arrangement of the Passengers' Luggage, etc.

Station Masters and Clerks. He is to take care that all the *servants* at his station come *on duty clean* in their persons and clothes, shaved and with their shoes brushed. He is also to cause the *Station to be kept clear* of weeds, and have the ballast raked and preserved in neat order.

Porters and Pointsmen. Every Pointsman on duty is to stand upon the line *clear of* the *rails* and to give the proper signal on the passing of an engine. Porters and Pointsmen generally are *not to allow* strangers to trespass on the line without written authority, and they are to report any occurrence of this nature to their Superior.

Gatemen at level crossings. Every Gateman will be provided with day and night *signals* which he must keep in proper order.

6 *Byelaws*

That if any Passenger or Passengers shall occupy (without permission) a superior class to that for which he has obtained a Ticket, or shall without permission continue his Journey in the Company's carriages beyond the place for which he shall have paid his Fare, he shall forfeit and pay the sum of 20 shillings, in addition to the Full Fare of the entire Journey.

For damage to the Company's property, a 20 shilling Fine and the costs of repairs.

N & CR Station Receipts and Expenses 1900

Station	Receipts £	Expenses £
Forth*	301,429	95,193
Elswick†	4,762	1,281
Scotswood	5,797	1,558
Blaydon	20,824	4,630
Ryton	4,196	363
Wylam	3,698	928
Prudhoe	5,818	893
Mickley†	95	——
Stocksfield	5,008	566
Riding Mill	2,054	395
Corbridge	6,651	704
Hexham	23,958	4,262
Fourstones	4,768	560
Haydon Bridge	2,974	671
Bardon Mill	1,876	310
Haltwhistle	7,453	1,168
Greenhead	2,327	211
Gilsland	2,106	596
Low Row	1,608	458
Naworth†	491	164
Brampton Jcn	5,216	1,014
How Mill	1,045	333
Heads Nook	1,910	298
Wetheral♮	2,505	664
Scotby	985	412
London Road*	16,454	9,126

* Goods traffic only handled.
† Passenger traffic only handled.
♮ Excludes Wetheral Bridge pedestrian tolls (usually over £150 per year).

APPENDIX 4

Passenger Traffic and Receipts 1951

Station	Passengers	Receipts £
Elswick	10,169	483
Scotswood	17,180	898
Blaydon	35,909	3,044
Lemington	12,799	490
Newburn	9,537	529
Heddon-on-the-Wall	2,428	68
North Wylam	37,197	1,957
Ryton	2,685	146
Wylam	30,261	2,033
Prudhoe	42,960	3,579
Stocksfield	18,055	2,026
Riding Mill	12,485	1,949
Corbridge	16,158	2,758
Hexham	70,683	18,668
Fourstones	4,349	753
Haydon Bridge	6,934	2,079
Haltwhistle	28,168	6,658
Greenhead	739	122
Gilsland	1,494	345
How Mill	2,890	229
Heads Nook	2,471	286
Wetheral	1,104	291
Scotby	506	57
Featherstone Park	4,653	205
Coanwood	12,469	651
Lambley	13,272	746
Slaggyford	5,657	523
Alston	6,279	1,604
Humshaugh	478	161
Reedsmouth	4,179	270
Bellingham (North Tyne)	6,589	947
Falstone	2,306	486
Kielder Forest	2,335	576
Deadwater	285	52

(Note: list of stations is incomplete)

199

APPENDIX 5

Locomotive Log; McDonnell 4–4–0 No 1494 on a Carlisle–Citadel–Newcastle (Blaydon) train*

DISTANCE miles		ACTUAL Min. Sec.	AVERAGE SPEEDS mph
0.0	CARLISLE	0.00	——
2.5	Scotby	5.15	28.5
4.3	Wetheral	7.17	52.9
6.0	Heads Nook	9.35	44.4
7.4	How Mill	12.01	34.5
10.8	Brampton Jcn.	18.57	——
1.6	Naworth	4.12	22.9
3.1	Low Row	6.17	43.2
6.9	Gilsland	10.57	48.9
5.3	HALTWHISTLE	8.20	——
4.7	Bardon Mill	6.40	——
8.8	Haydon Bridge	10.50	——
3.6	Fourstones	5.45	——
7.6	HEXHAM	10.43	——
3.1	Corbridge	5.33	33.5
5.4	Riding Mill	8.18	50.2
7.7	Stocksfield	11.28	44.0
10.2	Prudhoe	14.38	47.3
12.4	Wylam	17.18	49.6
14.6	Ryton	19.29	60.3
16.7	BLAYDON	22.58	——

(Train continued to Newcastle)

* From *Locomotives of the North Eastern Railway*, O.S. Nock, 1974 edn. (Ian Allan).

APPENDIX 6

Newcastle Tramways to Newburn

The *Newcastle Journal* of 30 July 1913 informed the public of the progress of the Corporation's electric tramway expansion in the western suburbs:

> Newburn Tram Extension—opening for traffic postponed. Colonel Von Donop on behalf of the Board of Trade yesterday inspected the tramways extension from the present Scotswood terminus to Sandy Banks, a short distance to the east of Newburn village. He was accompanied by Councillor J. H. Rodgers, Chairman of the Tramways Committee, Councillor Richard Mayne, Vice Chairman, Mr W. J. Steele, City Engineer, Mr Ernest Halton, General Manager of the Corporation Tramways, Mr Chalmers, Traffic Manager, (etc). The portion of the new track examined is about 2 miles in length. It connects the village of Bell's Close and Lemington with Newcastle and will also serve the residents of Newburn and adjacent villages. Ultimately the track will be extended to Throckley making it 3¾ miles long, but nearly 12 months will elapse it is expected, before this work is completed. Colonel Von Donop and the party who accompanied him travelled over the extension in a special car, particular attention being paid to the bridges spanning the route and other points where it is expected extra care will have to be exercised.

Then, on 2 August 1913:

> The new section of the Newcastle Corporation tramway system between Scotswood and Lemington was opened to the public yesterday. Shortly before 10 o'clock in the forenoon, a double decked car conveyed a full load of young folks.

The further extension to Newburn and Throckley soon followed.

APPENDIX 7

Closure of the Border Counties Railway—letters to the Editor, *Newcastle Journal*

19 October 1956.   Back to Stagecoach?

With the closing of the Hexham–Riccarton railway and all the complaining of the hardship of the people around Kielder, isn't it time someone gave a thought to the people in the other direction? What about the residents of Reedsmouth and district—Buteland Cottages, Broomhope Mill and the Steel, who have used the trains for years. Some have small babies and some are getting on in years and in poor health. They can't all afford taxis and haven't all the nerve to beg a lift in the school car. Can't they have some form of transport to and from the bus at Bellingham? Perhaps a covered wagon like Cecil Moffat ran at Kirkwhelpington in the good old days before this so-called progress. Even a stage coach, driven by the enterprising Mr Tommy Gilmour of Barrasford would be welcome.

(Mrs M. R. Tait, Reedsmouth)

I wonder why British Railways never tried running a couple of light steel diesel coaches capable of pulling 3 passenger coaches if necessary, on the North Tyne branch. It is a sheer lack of imagination to close one of the most beautiful routes in the north of England, that could have been developed into a tourist and scenic railway route. British Railways would perhaps do better to go back to the system of management on the old N.E. Railway, with local directors who took an interest in the North Tyne valley, instead of the present directorship from London, which does not understand the people living near the Borders.

(J. Thompson, Wallsend)

(Mr Thompson makes a minor error saying "N.E. Railway" in regard to the BCR).

APPENDIX 8

Last North Eastern Region Timetable, Newcastle to Carlisle line, 1967

Weekdays Down Service, from Newcastle Central.
00.30 (Carlisle, express), 05.30 (Hexham), 06.50 (Carlisle), 07.35 (Hexham), 08.15 SO (17 June–26 August, Heads of Ayr; 8 July–19 August, through carriage, Stranraer), 08.30 (Hexham),. 09.00 SO (8 July–26 August, Blackpool South), 09.20 (Carlisle), 09.50 (Hexham), 10.34 (Carlisle), 11.30 (Hexham), 12.30 (Carlisle), 13.40 (Hexham), 14.30 (Carlisle), 15.30 (Haltwhistle), 16.25 (Carlisle), 17.10 (Hexham), 17.40 (Carlisle), 18.20 (Carlisle), 19.10 (Hexham), 20.10 (Carlisle), 21.20 (Hexham), 22.10 (Hexham), 23.15 SX (Hexham), 23.15 SO (Carlisle), 23.45 FO (23 June–1 Sept. Stranraer Harbour).

Sundays Down Service.
10.00 (9 July–27 August, Carlisle), 11.20 (Carlisle), 12.50 (Hexham), 14.20 (Carlisle), 14.50 (Hexham), 15.50 (Hexham), 17.30 (Carlisle), 18.50 (Hexham), 20.20 (Carlisle), 22.25 (Hexham).

Weekdays Up Service, from Carlisle to Newcastle.
01.21 SO (29 July–19 August, from Stranraer Harbour, express), 02.50 (express), 07.30, 09.20, 11.14 SX (17 June–2 Sept.), 11.20 SO (17 June–2 Sept.), 13.14, 14.24, 16.20, 17.23 SO (24 June–2 Sept., from Stranraer Harbour), 18.25, 19.35, 19.45 SO (8 July–26 August), 21.20.

Sundays Up Service from Carlisle to Newcastle.
02.50 (express, but calls at Haltwhistle and Hexham by prior arrangement to set down passengers from N. Ireland), 11.00, 14.00, 17.00, 20.15.

Other up trains into Newcastle, with commencing stations.

Weekdays
06.20 (Hexham), 07.00 (Hexham), 07.13 (Haltwhistle), 08.00 (Hexham), 09.22 (Hexham), 11.00 (Hexham), 11.39 SO (Haltwhistle, through from Heads of Ayr, 17 June–2 Sept.), 13.00 (Hexham), 16.05 (Hexham), 18.00 (Hexham), 19.33 (Hexham), 21.20 (Hexham).

203

Sundays
13.50 (Hexham), 15.50 (Hexham), 16.50 (Hexham), 19.50 (Hexham). (Note, many trains routed via North Wylam including ALL Sunday trains, because of construction of new Scotswood Road bridge.)

Index

Page numbers in *italic* type denote illustrations